TAR

FOR EVERYONE

GW00357273

RICHARD WEBSTER

—ɱ—

TAROT FOR EVERYONE

by Richard Webster

Arcana from the Universal Tarot
Artwork by Roberto de Angelis

© Lo Scarabeo 2015

Lo Scarabeo
Via Cigna 110, 10155 - Torino, Italy
Tel: 011 283793 - Fax: 011 280756
E-mail: info@loscarabeo.com
Internet: http://www.loscarabeo.com
Facebook: LoScarabeoTarot

Printed by: Chenxy Printing

First edition: May 2015

All rights reserved.
No part of this book can be used or reproduced in any way – including publication on the
internet – without the express written consent of Lo Scarabeo, except in the case of brief
extracts to be used in reviews or critical articles.

TABLE OF CONTENTS

INTRODUCTION

The origins of the Tarot are lost in history. Although some people still claim it came from ancient Egypt, the Tarot probably originated in northern Italy in the early fifteenth century. Cards from the oldest existing decks date from between 1430 and 1450 and were made in Milan. The first almost complete deck in existence was designed by Bonifacio Bembo as a wedding gift for Francesco Sforza and Bianca Maria Visconti, members of the two noble families of Milan, in 1450. The Visconti family commissioned at least three Tarot decks in the 1440s, and fortunately, most of the cards from those decks still survive today.

The oldest known decks were painted by hand. The invention of printing made mass production of Tarot cards possible. The most famous of these early decks is the Tarot de Marseille, which is still used by many Tarot readers today. The biggest change in the Tarot deck occurred when the Rider-Waite-Smith Tarot deck was published in the United Kingdom in 1910. It was created by Arthur Edward Waite (1857–1942), a well-known occultist and writer, and Pamela Colman Smith (1878–1951), a professional artist. Their deck was the first one in modern times to include pictures on every card, making them much easier to learn and understand. Arthur Edward Waite had seen, or at least heard about, a fifteenth century Tarot deck called the Sola-Busca deck that contained illustrations on every card. Most decks published since the publication of the Rider-Waite-Smith deck include pictures on every card.

Since the late 1970s, more and more Tarot decks have become available, and many people enjoy collecting them. I have a large collection of Tarot decks, but the one I use most for professional purposes is the Universal Tarot. This is because the designs have similarities with those of the Rider-Waite-Smith Tarot, but are more modern looking and appeal to a contemporary audience. The pictures and symbols are clear and easy to read, making this the perfect deck for people who are new to the Tarot, and also for those who are reading the cards for others.

The origins of the Tarot are not known. As you learn more about the Tarot, you'll read a variety of opinions as to their origins. Arguably, the most popular myth about its origins dates back to 1781 when a French occultist, Antoine Court de Gébelin (1728-1784), published a book on ancient Egypt and claimed the Tarot deck was invented there. Other popular stories say the cards originated in Atlantis, China, India or Persia. One legend says the cards were created by a group of Cabalists in Morocco in the year 1300. For a long time people believed the Tarot was introduced into Europe by travelling Gypsies. However, this could not be the case as Tarot cards were being used in Italy well before the first Gypsies arrived there. Many people believe the cards were originally invented for a game called *Tarocchi*. Although it is not well known nowadays, a small number of people still play it today.

Many people have told me that the cards were not used for divination purposes until about one hundred and twenty years ago. They must have been disappointed when a manuscript dating back to 1750 was discovered that provided divinatory interpretations for each card, as well as methods for laying out the cards.

Today the Tarot is used as a tool for divination, for meditation purposes, and to help people grow spiritually. The reason the Tarot is still so popular today is that it is a useful tool that helps so many people. It provides useful, practical advice that will enable you to help other people as well as yourself. It provides a convenient way to connect your everyday life with the spiritual dimension. It encourages your intuition.

I'm sure you'll enjoy exploring the Tarot. You'll find it helpful, powerful and empowering. All you need is your imagination and a desire to learn. Be open minded, and trust that you already possess all the skills necessary to become a good Tarot card reader. The best approach is to relax, and have fun working with the cards. You don't need to try too hard. You'll find that more information will come to you when you're relaxed and receptive. Simply allow your subconscious mind to provide you with the insights you need.

Play with the cards. Study the pictures, and imagine what's going on in the different scenes. The body language and facial expressions of any person in the picture will provide helpful clues. Look at the setting, and the colours. I like to imagine myself inside the card, as this enables me to take part in whatever's going on, and I can use my imagination to have conversations with the people in the card. When you examine the cards, you'll probably find that some will instantly appeal to you, while others won't. This is good, as you can ask yourself why you feel a certain way with one card, and experience something completely different when looking at another one. Once you've looked at all the cards, you can start examining them in groups.

A good way to start is to lay out several cards in a line, and use your imagination to create a story using the pictures on the cards. If you need more cards to complete the story, continue dealing out as many cards as you need until the story comes to an end. When you start reading the cards for yourself and others, you'll deal them out in what's known as a "spread." As a spread is simply an arrangement of cards, dealing out the cards in a line is a form of spread.

Creating a story from the cards is exactly what you do when you read the cards. Usually, a question is asked, and the story created by the cards provides the answer. This isn't fortune-telling. The cards indicate possibilities, and what is likely to occur if you continue on your current path. The spread of cards provides additional information, and a different way of looking at the problem or concern. Consequently, after thinking about the information the cards have provided, you can continue on the path you're already on, or make any necessary changes.

How does the Tarot work? There are many theories, but no one knows. Carl Jung believed in synchronicity, or "meaningful coincidence." This means that although something appears to happen by chance, as everything in the universe is connected, the cards will somehow become arranged in an order that makes sense to the person asking the question. Consequently, when a question is asked, and a card selected, the card will relate to whatever the question happened to be.

Many people believe that some form of Divine intelligence controls the shuffling of the cards, and consequently, the cards that relate to the question appear in the spread. Others think that Tarot cards, and other tools such as rune stones and the I Ching, enable the reader to access parts of his or her subconscious mind and obtain information that could not be discovered by any other method. Another possible explanation is that the pictures and symbols on the Tarot cards enable our minds to look at problems in a different way, and they trigger the subconscious mind to provide solutions that would not have occurred to us otherwise.

Most Tarot card readers don't worry about how it works, as they know that the images and symbolism of each card, combined with their own intuition, enables them to look at any situation from a different point of view, and find a satisfactory resolution.

—m—

COMMON MISCONCEPTIONS

Finally, before we start examining each card in depth, I'd like to remove four misconceptions that people often have about the Tarot.

The first of these is that there's a huge amount of memorization required. This isn't the case. You don't have to remember everything I say about the cards in this book. The illustrations provide plenty of information, and you'll gradually learn more as you work with the cards. After describing the cards, I've included a chapter on ways to help you remember the cards.

The second misconception is that you need to be highly intuitive to read the cards. Again, this is not the case. Your intuition will grow as you work with the cards, but you don't need a huge amount of psychic ability to be a good reader.

The third misconception is that reading cards for other people is exhausting and drains you of energy. It can be, if you put unnecessary pressure on yourself. If you claim to be an amazing oracle who "knows all, and sees all" you'll quickly become stressed out and exhausted, as you're putting all the responsibility for a successful reading on yourself. However, if you approach the reading as a conversation between two people, in which you explore the situation and put forward possible solutions, you'll find you'll gain energy, rather than lose it.

The fourth misconception is that you must read the Tarot for others. I know many people who read the Tarot for themselves, and seldom - if ever - read the cards for anyone else. I enjoy reading the Tarot for other people, and consider it a privilege to be able to do so, but I use the cards for myself much more frequently than I do for other people. Most people read the cards for themselves and for friends and family, and derive a great deal of pleasure and satisfaction from being able to help the people they care about. However, I also know people who read the cards solely for themselves, and in some cases haven't told anyone else about their interest in the subject. It's entirely up to you what you do with your cards.

—⁓—

FIRST THINGS FIRST

The Tarot deck contains 78 cards that are divided two distinct sections: the Major and Minor Arcanas. The 22 cards of the Major Arcana are numbered from 0 (The Fool) to XXI (The World). These cards symbolize the most important issues of our lives, such as turning points, milestones and lessons learned. The 56 cards of the Minor Arcana are divided into four suits, each containing 14 cards. These are the suits of Chalices, Pentacles, Wands and Swords. In each suit there are ten pip cards, numbered from 1 to 10. There are also four Court cards in each suit: the Knave, the Knight, the Queen, and the King. The cards of the Minor Arcana symbolize everyday situations, circumstances, experiences, and the inevitable ups and downs of life. The Court cards represent the people in our lives, but can also reveal aspects of our own personalities, and the energies surrounding a particular situation.

The four suits are associated with the four ancient elements of Fire, Earth, Air and Water. These four elements have been used for at least 2,500 years to symbolize different categories of life, and they are used in magic and astrology as well as the Tarot. Aries, Leo and Sagittarius, for instance, are associated with the element of Fire. People born into these signs are fiery, enthusiastic and romantic. Taurus, Virgo and Capricorn are associated with Earth. People born into these signs are practical, reliable, down-to-earth, and enjoy their material comforts. Gemini, Libra and Aquarius are associated with Air. People born into these signs are logical, idealistic, and good communicators. Cancer, Scorpio and Pisces are associated with Water. People born into these signs are emotional, intuitive and receptive.

Each suit relates to a specific area of life, which is determined by the element the suit belongs to:

- The **Chalices (Water)** relate to love, relationships, emotions, feelings, pleasure and intuition.
- The **Pentacles (Earth)** relate to manifestation, the material world, money, career, security and power.
- The **Wands (Fire)** relate to creativity, ideas, action, ambition, expansion and growth.
- The **Swords (Air)** relate to conflicts, difficulties, sorrow and ill health.

MAJOR ARCANA

The 22 cards of the Major Arcana are the most important cards in the deck. In fact, "Major Arcana" means "big secret." They represent important aspects of human experience, such as the significant milestones and events, as well as the highs and lows, and the hopes and ambitions, of a person's life. If a spread of cards contains a larger than usual number of Major Arcana cards, you can safely assume that the person involved, or the matter concerned, is deeper and more profound than usual.

As we go through life, we all experience each card of the Major Arcana. However, we do not necessarily go through the Major Arcana in card order.

I have included the element and astrological association for each card in the Major Arcana. This is because many people who take up the Tarot have already studied astrology, and find these associations helpful. However, the Tarot cards stand on their own, and you need no knowledge of astrology to become a good reader. Use the astrological associations if you find them helpful. If you know nothing about astrology, pay no attention to them.

If a card appears reversed, or upside down, in a spread, it can indicate a different meaning to when it's upright. This optional technique is discussed later, but you will also find suggestions for the reversed meaning in the description of each Arcana.

—⚉—

0. THE FOOL

Element: Air
Astrological association: Uranus
Description: The Fool card shows a carefree young man walking towards the edge of a precipice. He is high up in the mountains, and is looking ahead, rather than at the imminent danger at his feet. A dog is following close behind, and appears to be trying to warn the young man of the dangers ahead. The Fool carries a wand on his right shoulder. This symbolizes will. Hanging from the wand is a satchel containing all the wisdom of the world. In his left hand he carries a rose that symbolizes innocence.

The Fool is about to start something new, or to head in a new direction. There are likely to be new plans, fresh ideas, and new people in the Fool's life. He is idealistic, innocent, carefree, spontaneous and uncompromising. He has an original, even slightly eccentric, approach, which is why he's associated with the planet Uranus. Uranus is the only planet that rotates horizontally on its axis as it circles around the Sun, out of step with all the other planets.

The Fool may sound immature and frivolous, but he is more complex than he first appears. The Fool represents all of us, as we're all innocents when we start something new, or are placed into a new environment or situation. The Fool represents the potential that lies in every situation. We might feel excited, exhilarated and happy to make this new start. Conversely, we might feel vulnerable, scared, or fearful, especially if the new beginnings have been forced upon us.

The Fool represents possibilities. This potential means little until a decision is made, and you make your first step. This is followed by another, and another, and soon you'll be feeling comfortable on your new path.

Reversed: Be cautious, and check your plans carefully before proceeding. Avoid unnecessary risks. You might be careless, negligent, or overly naïve. Expect delays, confusion and problems.

—∿—

I. THE MAGICIAN

Element: Air

Astrological Association: Mercury

Description: The Magician stands in a pastoral scene with his right hand pointing heavenwards, and his left hand pointing down to the earth. This shows that he's gaining power from heaven and directing it into the material world. On the table in front of him are a wand, cup, sword and pentacle. These symbolize the elements of Fire, Water, Air and Earth. The roses and lilies in the garden show that he can nurture anything he desires. The figure eight, lying on its side, above the Magician's head is called a lemniscate. It symbolizes eternal life.

The Magician represents skill. He is confident, masterful, powerful, wise and diplomatic. He has the ability to focus his will on anything he desires and make it happen.

Reversed: This is a sign that someone is not as honest or sincere as they appear. Someone might be two-faced and be secretly working against you. Think things through, listen to your hunches and feelings, and trust yourself.

—ⱳ—

II. THE HIGH PRIESTESS

Element: Water
Astrological Association: Moon
Description: The High Priestess sits on a throne with a crescent moon at her feet. She holds a scroll labelled Tora (divine laws). It is partially hidden by the green robe the High Priestess is wearing. This shows that only half of the mystery can be understood. She sits between two pillars. The black one, labelled B for Boaz, indicates the negative side of life, while the white one, J for Jakin, represents the positive potential. The cross on her chest also indicates positivity and negativity. Behind the High Priestess is a veil decorated with palms and pomegranates. These are male and female symbols, and indicate subconscious potential.

The High Priestess indicates a future that is yet to be revealed. It suggests listening to your subconscious mind for the wisdom that is hidden inside. There are unknown influences working behind the scenes. Listen to your dreams, and trust your intuition.

Reversed: Be patient, allow whatever time is necessary, and don't try to force anything to happen. There is the possibility of deceit, manipulation, and hidden agendas. Don't take everything at face value, listen to what other people have to say, but make up your own mind on anything important that relates to you and your loved ones.

—⚌—

III. THE EMPRESS

Element: Venus
Astrological Association: Earth
Description: The Empress is sitting in a beautiful garden, symbolizing fertility and creativity. The heart-shaped shield by her side indicates Venus, the goddess of love. The Empress appears to be pregnant.

The Empress indicates fruitfulness, creativity, nurturing, and understanding. It can indicate fertility and the birth of something new. It is a good card for relationships, and relates strongly to motherhood and children. It also indicates creativity, good fortune, and material rewards.

Reversed: You may feel lazy, unmotivated, blocked and resentful. It may seem as if nothing is working and it's a waste of time to even try. Be patient, and start making plans for the future.

—ɯɯ—

IV. THE EMPEROR

Element: Fire
Astrological Association: Aries
Description: The Emperor sits on a throne. Rams' heads are depicted on the arms and back of the throne. These symbolize the sign of Aries. In his right hand he holds a wand in the shape of a stylized ankh, which is the Egyptian symbol of life. Behind him, in the distance, are bleak-looking mountains, indicating the barrenness of uncompromising power.

The Emperor and Empress are not necessarily a couple. The Emperor symbolizes logic and thought, rather than the intuition and access to the subconscious possessed by the Empress. He is intellectual, rather than emotional. The Emperor signifies leadership, authority, stability, responsibility, ambition, action, power and respect. This card can indicate that an older man in a position of authority is prepared to help you.

Reversed: Someone (possibly you) is proving rigid, stubborn and inflexible right now. This is a challenging time, and you'll find it hard to progress. You may feel as if you're taking two steps backwards, to every step forward. You must remain focused and determined to achieve your goals.

—ɯ—

V. THE HIEROPHANT

Element: Earth

Astrological Association: Taurus

Description: The Hierophant is seated on a throne between two pillars. This is similar to the pose of the High Priestess, the card he is paired with. He holds a staff with a triple cross. His right hand makes a sign of peace. At his feet are the crossed keys to the kingdom. They can unlock the gates to both Heaven and Hell. This relates to the opposites of good and evil, male and female, the Sun and the Moon, and the conscious and subconscious minds. Before him kneel two initiates.

The High Priestess gains wisdom through experience, the Hierophant learns his through logic and study. The Hierophant indicates structured organisations, tradition, conventional wisdom, and the church. This card also indicates a teacher, mentor or knowledgeable person who can offer advice and help.

Reversed: This is a sign of intolerance, domination and fear. Someone is abusing their power and trying to hold you back. Take time out, and return to your daily routine with a fresh point of view. You may find that an unconventional approach will help you resolve your problems at this time.

—⚡—

VI. THE LOVERS

Element: Air

Astrological Association: Gemini

Description: The Lovers card shows a man and a woman standing in front of two trees. Archangel Raphael is gazing down on them. The man stands before the Tree of Life, and the woman stands in front of the Tree of the Knowledge of Good and Evil. This tree has a snake entwined around it. Early versions of this card usually showed a man making a choice between two women. Consequently, as well as being a card of love, the Lovers also indicates choice, and the responsibility that comes with making a decision.

The Lovers card signifies romantic love, and the choices that have to be made within the relationship. It is also a card of beauty, attraction, affection, communication and partnership.

Reversed: This is a sign of difficulties within a relationship. Consequently, it relates to bad choices, suspicion, jealousy, infidelity, miscommunication, separation, breakups and endings. It can also indicate immaturity and a fear of commitment.

—ᜠ—

VII. THE CHARIOT

Element: Water

Astrological Association: Cancer

Description: The Chariot card shows a princely figure standing in a chariot drawn by two sphinxes that signify positive and negative energy. The whit sphinx symbolizes mercy, while the black sphinx depicts justice. The fact that the sphinxes are pulling in different directions emphasizes the conflict between these two energies. The figure in the chariot signifies earthly power, and the stars in the canopy above him indicate heavenly power.

The Chariot card means progress, success, triumph over difficulties, assertiveness, balancing opposing energies, travel, willpower and determination. It's a time to accept new opportunities and to move forward with resolution and a strong sense of purpose.

Reversed: This relates to conflicts, disappointments, rejections, delays, opposition, lack of focus, and lack of commitment. You're likely to feel a lack of energy and have a sense that you've lost your way, and are no longer in control of your own of your own destiny. Lessen your workload, and learn to say "no" when people try to increase your workload.

—w—

VIII. STRENGTH

Element: Fire

Astrological Association: Leo

Description: The Strength card shows a young woman closing the mouth of a lion. Over her head is the lemniscate that we saw in the Magician card. This is the symbol of eternal life. The picture of someone overcoming the king of beasts symbolizes man's struggle to overcome his innate animal instincts. The strength of this card is not just physical strength, but inner strength as well.

The Strength card symbolizes gentleness, patience, courage, endurance, acceptance, compassion, confidence, determination, wisdom and self-awareness. You'll be able to resolve any longstanding problems with ease at this time. Accept others as they are, and be kind to yourself.

Reversed: This is a sign of weakness, fear, shyness, timidity, holding back, and lack of self-esteem. It can also indicate depression and health problems. Make sure you're getting enough rest, avoid artificial stimulants, and keep on top of your thinking.

—ɯ—

IX. THE HERMIT

Element: Earth

Astrological Association: Virgo

Description: The Hermit is standing on a mountaintop holding a lantern that illuminates his path. In his left hand he holds a staff, which is a well known sign of healing. It shows that the pursuit of knowledge enables one to become whole.

The Hermit card indicates a period of introspection, solitude, contemplation, study, wisdom, knowledge and guidance. You'll feel the need to spend time on your own to think matters through. It's the card of "patient waiting," which is never easy to do. This is a good time to consult with others, and to learn different points of view. It's also a good time to study anything that appeals to you.

Reversed: This is a sign to slow down and listen to your inner voice. It can also indicate introversion, loneliness, isolation, lack of human contact, and a feeling of being totally alone in an uncaring world. Make sure that your negative feelings don't force the special people in your life away, as this is the time when you really need them.

—◆—

X. THE WHEEL

Element: Fire

Astrological Association: Jupiter

Description: The Wheel card shows a rotating wheel floating in space, surrounded by the four mystical animals of the Bible (Ezekiel 1:10). These relate to the fixed signs of the zodiac. The bull at the bottom left relates to the sign of Taurus, the Lion to its right relates to Leo, the eagle at the top right relates to Scorpio, and the angel at the top left relates to Aquarius. They all symbolize the fact that nothing changes despite the constant revolutions of the wheel. The zodiac itself is a wheel. There are also three figures on the wheel itself. They depict Egyptian gods: Anubis, the jackal-headed god who conducted souls, Seth, the snake god, and the sphinx who represents Horus, the god of resurrection. They symbolize the transition from death to rebirth. The Letters on the wheel can spell either TARO or ROTA, which is Latin for wheel.

The Wheel relates to change, the one constant in life. More important than the change, though, is how we react to it. The Wheel relates to good fortune, luck, opportunity, advancement, fate and success. Everything is going your way right now. Expect good things to happen and make the most of the opportunities that come your way.

Reversed: This position indicates the opposite of good luck. Consequently, there'll be delays and frustrations, failures, unexpected setbacks, and a sense of loss of control. Be cautious, and wait for conditions to improve when the wheel of fortune turns again.

—ɯ—

XI. JUSTICE

Element: Air
Astrological Association: Libra
Description: Justice is a female figure who sits between two pillars with a sword in her right hand and a set of scales in her left. The scales relate to a carefully balanced judgment, and the sword is double-edged, which means it can cut two ways. This shows that justice occurs as a result of past actions. The pillars also represent balance between two opposites.

Justice is completely impartial. When something is out of balance, this card corrects the situation. This card relates to karma, fair play, truth, integrity, fairness, legal matters, arbitration, contracts, rational thought, decisions, and correct outcomes. If you act with honesty and integrity, and deliberate carefully before making decisions, everything will go your way. It's important that you act fairly and honestly. If you do, justice will always prevail.

Reversed: Life won't seem fair at this time. This placement relates to dishonesty, injustice, deception, hidden enemies, and a feeling of hopelessness. You'll experience more than your share of delays and frustrations. Act honourably, no matter what other people are doing.

—ɯ—

XII. THE HANGED MAN

Element: Water

Astrological Association: Neptune

Description: The Hanged Man is suspended from a gibbet made from living wood. His folded arms create a triangle behind his back, and his legs form the shape of a cross. He has a halo around his head. Rather than discomfort, the Hanged Man appears to be serene and perfectly at peace. He is looking at life from a different perspective to gain greater spiritual understanding.

The Hanged Man indicates that a sacrifice needs to be made. It's a testing time and something worthwhile has to be given up for something that is worth considerably more. This card relates to spirituality, wisdom, selflessness, self-sacrifice, transition, suspension, limbo, a different point of view and an unconventional approach.

Reversed: The Hanged Man reversed is actually upright. This can be a good sign, showing that a difficult time is almost over and you'll be able to start moving forward again. However, in the present you may be living according to other people's expectations and feel unable to commit to what you really want to do. This leads only to dissatisfaction, depression and a sense of failure.

XIII. DEATH

Element: Water
Astrological Association: Scorpio
Description: Death, wearing a suit of armour, is riding a white horse across a damaged landscape. He is holding a black banner containing a Mystic Rose, which is a symbol of life. This rose contains five petals that represent the four elements and the spirit of life. In the background, the sun is shining between two towers that symbolize the duality of life. In the middle distance, a boat can be seen on a river, presumably the River Styx that marks the boundary between Earth and the Underworld. Nothing can withstand Death, and the card shows people falling powerless before him. Under the horse's hooves is the body of a king, and in front of it is a bishop who stands, waiting for Death.

Death is the card that frightens most people. However, it does not necessarily mean physical death. It means the death or ending of something that is old, outmoded, and has ceased to have any purpose in your life.

The Death card means transformation, death, rebirth, endings, transformation, changes, and the end of anything that is no longer relevant or useful. All of this clears away everything that has been holding you back, and you'll start looking at all the wonderful opportunities that are in front of you.

Reversed: This can indicate stubbornness, fear of change, and a reluctance to let go of something. It's literally hanging on to the past. You won't be able to move forward until you let go of your negative thoughts and feelings.

—ⅲ—

XIV. TEMPERANCE

Element: Fire
Astrological Association: Sagittarius
Description: A winged angel stands with one foot on dry land and the other in water. This symbolizes continuity. He is pouring liquid from one chalice to another. The flowers are irises, named after the Greek goddess Iris who delivered messages from heaven to earth using rainbows as a bridge. As a rainbow was sent by God after the great flood, rainbows have become a symbol of peace and the promise of rebirth and continuity. The Sun in the background indicates a new dawn. The stream the angel is standing in indicate the past, present and future.

Temperance suggests moderation in all things. It relates to modification, adaptability, self-control, patience, tolerance, compromise, harmony, forgiveness and open communication. You may need to pause for a while to re-evaluate the course of your life. All your dealings with others are good, though you may need to compromise at times.

Reversed: This is a sign that you're trying to do much more than your fair share. Pause, re-evaluate, and decide what it is you really want to do. Work hard, but remember to take sufficient time off for rest and relaxation. However, you may need to avoid excesses, inappropriate behaviour, overindulgence, and temptation.

—ɯ—

XV. THE DEVIL

Element: Earth

Astrological Association: Capricorn

Description: The Devil, a horned being with bat-like wings, sits on a half-cube laughing at a naked man and woman who are chained by the neck to the half-cube. An inverted pentagram between the Devil's horns show that reality has been turned upside down. The half-cube shows that only half of mankind's potential is being utilised. The chains confining the man and the woman are so loose they could easily be removed. This shows that most of their bondage is not real. This card can be seen as the opposite of card #VI: The Lovers, as the two human figures are the same in both cards.

The Devil is usually viewed as a negative figure, but this is not necessarily the case. He represents the baser, darker, more materialistic and physical sides of our natures. When utilized properly, these urges for immediate pleasure and gratification can be harnessed into creative activities that enhance our lives.

The Devil signifies bondage, materialism, violence, lust, obsession, guilt, and the unknown. However, it also provides the ability to remove the blocks that hold us back from achieving our potential. You're likely to be feeling trapped right now, and it's likely to be your own fault as you've become a slave to materialism, negative thoughts and difficult, stress-producing relationships. You need to face your fears, and let go of whatever is causing the problem.

Reversed: The Devil can be a positive card in this placement as it enables you to release the chains, overcome the present situation, reclaim your own personal power, and start living again. However, it can also indicate greed, selfishness, and self indulgence.

—ɷ—

XVI. THE TOWER

Element: Fire

Astrological Association: Mars

Description: The Tower has been struck by lightning and flames can be seen through the windows and top of the tower. A man and a woman have leapt off the tower in an attempt to save themselves. The lightning represents divine power. This card shows that something in the person's life has become so restricting that it needs to be exploded before further growth can take place. We all resist change, and this experience forces that change upon us. Although this experience can be shattering and dramatic, an important lesson will be learned and false beliefs will be seen for what they truly are. These provide the person with a new sense of freedom, and the opportunity to start anew on a fresh and different path.

The Tower signifies sudden, unexpected change, catastrophe, upheaval, catharsis, conflict, disruption and the end of an existing way of life. Expect the unexpected.

Reversed: This placement shows that you need to overcome your fear of change, and look at it as an opportunity, rather than a threat. Because of past mistakes there could be problems and difficulties in the short term. You'll be able to deal with these effectively, and start working on deliberate changes that will help you get where you want to go.

—⚏—

XVII. THE STARS

Element: Air

Astrological Association: Aquarius

Description: A young woman kneels beside a pond, with one foot in the water. She pours the Waters of Life from two jugs onto the earth and into the pool of water. This pool symbolizes universal consciousness, and the earth signifies matter. Behind her is the tree of life with an Ibis standing on it. The ibis was considered sacred by the ancient Egyptians and it came to symbolize the ability of the soul to grow and develop. In the sky is a large eight-pointed star surrounded by seven smaller stars. All of these represent the four elements. There is Water in the pool, the bird symbolizes Air, the flowers and trees represent Earth, and the stars symbolize divine Fire.

The phrase "wish upon a star" means something when this card appears in a spread. It's one of two wish cards in the Tarot deck, and you should make a wish whenever it appears. (The Nine of Chalices is the other wish card.)

The Star card symbolizes hope, inspiration, renewal, guidance, protection, optimism, serenity, happiness, good luck, joy and faith in the future. This is an extremely fortunate card, and you should use this positive time to make progress towards your goals. It's also a good time to act on your intuition and to develop spiritually.

Reversed: This is a sign of indecisiveness, hopelessness, disappointment, doubt and discouragement. It's not much fun wallowing in self pity, and it's entirely up to you when you decide to adopt a more positive attitude again.

XVIII. THE MOON

Element: Water

Astrological Association: Pisces

Description: The full Moon looks down upon a pool, out of which a crayfish is emerging. This symbolizes birth and the earliest stage of consciousness. Two dogs are in the foreground, one looking into the pond and the other gazing at the moon. A path leads from the pond into the far distance. The two towers symbolize good and evil. The moon is associated with dreams and the subconscious mind. Consequently, the path in this card is sometimes called "the road of dreams." The two dogs symbolize the animal side of our natures. When this card appears in a spread it's usually a sign that something is proving difficult or confusing, and needs time to sort itself out. Refuse to listen to gossip or rumours, and spend as much time as you can with positive people.

The Moon card symbolizes confusion, illusion, secrets, deception, imagination, fluctuating emotions, uncertainty and creativity. It also symbolizes hunches, feelings, intuition and the subconscious mind. It's a sign that something that's been secret or hidden is becoming more apparent, and you will need to attend to whatever it is before proceeding. Pay special attention to your dreams, hunches and feelings, as they are likely to prove more useful that cold, hard logic.

Reversed: This is a sign that the road ahead is becoming easier for you. Something that held you back will no longer have any meaning to you, and you'll view the present situation with fresh eyes. Trust your intuition.

—ɯ—

XIX. THE SUN

Element: Fire

Astrological association: Sun

Description: A naked child rides a white horse inside a walled garden. Overhead, the Sun sends warming rays onto the scene. The rays alternate between straight and wavy lines. This shows the duality of the Sun. The Sun's fiery rays can warm, brighten and ripen, but can also do the opposite by parching and ultimately killing plants and crops. The sunflowers turn their heads to follow the Sun. A large banner rises heavenward from behind the horse.

The Sun is a happy, joyful card. It symbolizes happiness, success, achievement, celebration, contentment, fulfilment, optimism, enthusiasm, confidence, friendship, energy and an improvement in all areas of life. It's an extremely positive card, and you should celebrate your good fortune with friends and family.

Reversed: The Sun in this placement indicates a disappointment or setback. You're not being fully appreciated, and someone else may get credit for what you've done. Success is so close you can almost taste it, but you'll have to wait just a little bit longer for it to happen.

—ɯ—

XX. JUDGEMENT

Element: Fire

Astrological Association: Pluto

Description: It is the Day of Judgement, and Archangel Gabriel (some people say Archangel Michael) has emerged from the heavens and is blowing his trumpet, calling the dead to arise. On the ground, coffins have opened and people are waking up from their long sleep. In the foreground, a man, a woman and a child gaze up towards the angel in adoration. Judgement indicates rebirth. It enables forgiveness and healing to occur, as we let go of past grievances and start anew.

Judgement symbolizes awakening, rebirth, learning from experience, forgiveness and karma. Nothing can stop you now. Think carefully, and then act. This card is a strong indication that you're coming to the end of a cycle of experience and need to start thinking and planning for the stage of your life. Enjoy the rewards of your hard work, and prepare for more success in the future.

Reversed: This is a time to re-evaluate what you're doing and where you want to go. You may still be holding on to grievances from the past, experiencing remorse, or having doubts about your capabilities. There could be changes that are out of your control. There will be delays, but they won't last long.

—ɯ—

XXI. THE WORLD

Element: Earth

Astrological Association: Saturn

Description: A dancer is encircled by a wreath of laurel leaves, a symbol of achievement and success. She holds a wand in each hand. In the four corners of the card are the four animals mentioned in Ezekiel. (They also appear in Card #X: The Wheel.) This is the final card in the Major Arcana, and it symbolizes completion and attainment. It marks the end of an important cycle in your life. The dancer is celebrating her success before being reborn as The Fool and starting the cycle again. This is inevitable as, as soon as you've achieved something, you start thinking about new opportunities and challenges.

The World card symbolizes success, achievement, attainment, completion, accomplishment, fulfillment, celebration and – sometimes – travel. You'll receive your reward for everything you achieved during this cycle. Enjoy celebrating your success, take some time off, and then start work on your next major goal.

Reversed: A cycle is coming to an end, but you'll feel frustrated because there'll be delays, setbacks, and possibly a loss before you can start on a new cycle. There'll be some unfinished business that needs to be attended to before you can achieve your goals.

MINOR ARCANA

The cards of the Major Arcana depict the important, overriding themes of our lives. The Major Arcana cards usually deal with profound matters that relate to the person's inner growth and development. The Minor Arcana reveal the everyday concerns of our lives. The Minor Arcana consists of fifty-six cards, divided into four suits, each containing fourteen cards. There are ten numbered cards and four court cards. The court cards usually indicate important people in the sitter's life, but can also reveal some of his or her own attributes, which can be unknown. Each suit relates to one of the four elements of fire, earth, air and water.

You'll notice that seasons of the years are included for some of the cards. This is usually a guide for timing when events are likely to occur. However, it can also indicate a sense of the feelings created by the card. Thoughts and feelings about the season of Spring, for instance, are quite different to those about Winter.

—ɯ—

THE SUIT OF CHALICES

The Suit of Chalices relates to emotions and situations that involve love, friendship, personal relationships, sensitivity, fulfilment, fantasy, emotions, feelings, intuition, creativity and spirituality. The Chalices relate to the Water signs of the zodiac: Cancer, Scorpio and Pisces. The Chalices relate to the suit of Hearts in a deck of regular playing cards.

ACE of CHALICES

Season: None

Description: A hand holding a chalice emerges from a cloud. Four streams of water pour out of the chalice and fall into the waters below. A dove is flying into the chalice and appears to be about to drop a wafer with a cross on it into the cup.

All the aces of the Minor Arcana relate to creative potential, new beginnings, and a time for the person to take action. The Ace of Chalices is an excellent card as it relates to emotional fulfilment inside a relationship, which may be new or existing. It marks the start of a happy, productive stage of life. This usually involves family and loved ones, but it can also indicate the start of some form of creativity, and new spiritual insights. It also relates to joy, healing, abundance, compassion and strong emotions.

Reversed: This is not an easy placement. When the Ace of Chalices is reversed it signifies unrequited love, a broken heart, separation, loneliness, animosity, and regrets. Think carefully before speaking, and keep calm, no matter what is going on around you.

2 of CHALICES

Season: Winter

Description: A young couple gaze into each other's eyes as they toast their relationship. Above the cups they are holding is a caduceus, which was the staff carried by Hermes in Greek mythology. This relates to the merging of masculine and feminine energies. The caduceus appears to be supported by a lion's head with two wings, that again relate to male and female.

The Two of Chalices relates to compatibility and emotional harmony. It usually indicates the start of a relationship. This could be a love affair, or possibly an engagement or marriage. It could mean falling in love at first sight. It can also indicate harmonious relationships of all sorts, such as a close friendship or a business partnership.

Reversed: This is a sign of problems in a relationship. There could be scenes, arguments, rejection, broken trust, and the possibility of a break-up. If you want to save the relationship, act quickly, and have a serious heart to heart discussion about everything that's bothering you.

3 of CHALICES

Season: First signs of Spring

Description: Three young women raise their cups high to pledge their love and friendship for each other. They have flowers in their hair, and appear to be dancing in a vineyard. They symbolize joy and happiness.

The Three of Chalices relates to appreciating the special people in our lives. It can indicate a celebration or special event, but is more likely to represent a casual party or social gathering. It relates to friendship, family, fun, living in the present moment and abundance.

Reversed: You may feel left out, ignored, or forgotten. Apologize, if you've done anything wrong. Spend time on your own thinking about all the good things in your life. If you count your blessings, the current, temporary situation won't seem as bad as you think. A reversed Three of Chalices can also indicate overindulgence, promiscuity and excess.

4 of CHALICES

Season: Spring

Description: A young woman sits on the ground in front of a tree. There are three cups in front of her. A hand emerges from a cloud and offers her another cup, but she remains discontented.

The Four of Chalices relates to stubbornness, boredom, dissatisfaction and withdrawal. You may desire a change, but feel frustrated and reluctant to start anything new. The message is that you should make the most of everything you can in the present moment, rather than worrying about what may or may not occur in the future. You should look for the positive, rather than dwelling on the negative. This card also relates to depression, lack of gratitude, and re-evaluation.

Reversed: You are likely to have strong feelings about someone, or a situation, right now. Try to keep a positive mental attitude. Avoid taking sides, and spend time working on resolving the problem. This card reversed can also be a sign that everything in your life is slowly starting to improve.

5 of CHALICES

Season: Late Spring and Early Summer

Description: A young man in a dark cloak looks at three fallen cups. As he is focussed on these, he fails to notice the two standing cups behind him. In the background a bridge crosses a river and provides access to a small castle where he presumably lives.

• The Five of Chalices relates to the old question: *Is your cup half full or half empty?* This card relates to regrets, dissatisfactions, lack of fulfilment, disappointment, frustration, bitterness, and temporary failure. You may be feeling sorry for yourself because matters didn't work out the way they were intended. To move ahead again, you need to let go of the past and learn from any mistakes that were made.

Reversed: You may be feeling sad and sorry for yourself. Be prepared to let go of anyone or anything that has run its course, and start looking ahead. Your situation is improving, and there's no need to wallow in despair. Mourn by all means, and then move on.

6 of CHALICES

Season: Summer

Description: Two children are filling their cups with flowers outside a beautiful home. The boy is handing a cup full of flowers to the young girl. They are playing happily and enjoying their innocent pleasures.

This is a card of nostalgia. It's looking back at happy memories from the past. It's good to reminisce and enjoy thinking about the past, but we can live only in the present. This card indicates a time of creativity, play, and an absence of adult responsibilities. Time out can be restorative and healing, and once you've had your rest, you can start moving forward again. The Six of Chalices can also indicate naïvety, and a need to think more seriously about the current situation.

Reversed: This is a sign that you're clinging to the past, and are finding it hard to make plans for the future. We can remember the past, and look forward to the future, but we can live only in the present. Be grateful for the blessings in your life, and take one or two small steps forward. It might seem hard to believe right now, but your future is going to be much better than you think.

7 of CHALICES

Season: Late Summer and Early Autumn

Description: A man is gazing at seven cups floating on a cloud. They are all full of illusions. There's a castle, a snake, a laurel crown, jewelry, a dragon, a woman's head and a figure that looks as if it's risen from the dead. These are all illusions, or castles in the air.

The Seven of Chalices is a card of temptation and greed. The person has too many different and opposing ideas, and his or her energies are scattered. This card relates to confusion, lack of focus, fantasies, and too much choice. Consequently, even though the person has the necessary skills and talent, he or she is confused and doesn't know which way to turn.

Reversed: Think carefully before acting, and take advice from people you trust. If you set worthwhile goals for yourself, and work hard, you'll be successful. However, you're likely to make mistakes if you jump in before finding out all the facts.

8 of CHALICES

Season: Autumn

Description: A man walks away from the cups that previously provided happiness and satisfaction. The cups are arranged in two layers, with five on the bottom and three on top. One of the top three is set apart from the others. As this is the suit of emotions, this indicates a loss, probably of love or friendship. The man is using a staff, which indicates he is going to be travelling a long way. He is leaving the past behind.

The Eight of Chalices is a card of upheaval and disappointment. It indicates a time to let go of something that is no longer working, and to search for a new way to move forward again. This can also indicate a time to pause and reflect on what's going on in your life.

Reversed: This is a time to pause and reflect. Accept others as they are, avoid making excuses, and refuse to be pushed into anything you don't want to do. Use this quiet time to think about what is going on in your life, and what changes you would like to make to help create a better future.

9 of CHALICES

Season: Late Autumn and Early Winter

Description: A large man appearing satisfied with his life is sitting on a large stool. Behind him are nine chalices, symbolizing the opulence of his lifestyle. This card is traditionally known as the "wish" card, as when it appears something the person has longed for may become a reality.

The Nine of Chalices relates to pride, emotional satisfaction, fulfilment, worldly pleasures, satisfaction and material success. The Nine of Chalices is one of the most positive cards in the Tarot deck, and you'll feel peaceful and contented in every area of your life.

Reversed: This is a time for caution. Allow matters to take as long as necessary. You'll probably be disappointed if you try to force things to go the way you want. Be generous, help others, and focus on what you can give, rather than what you can take.

10 of CHALICES

Season: All

Description: Two people, presumably husband and wife, look upward at a beautiful rainbow of ten cups. In front of them two children are playing, and in the middle distance is a house in a pleasant green landscape.

The Ten of Chalices represents a time of happiness and contentment. It is a time to enjoy the rewards of all the effort that has been made in the past. This card symbolizes good fortune that has been earned.

This card relates to peace, harmony, tranquillity, happiness, good luck, successful family life, love, affection, friendship, prosperity, and the attainment of worthwhile goals.

Reversed: Your attitude is more than usually important right now. There's the possibility of arguments and disharmony amongst friends and family, and you may need to step in and soothe the situation.

—៱៱—

THE SUIT OF PENTACLES

The Suit of Pentacles relates to the element of Earth. In an ordinary deck of playing cards, this element is represented by the suit of diamonds. In ancient times, the Earth was considered a goddess, and was often called "Mother Earth." Earth is feminine and receptive. It symbolizes the physical body and the everyday, tangible, material world. At its most basic, this is money. The Pentacles relate to the Earth signs of Taurus, Virgo and Capricorn.

ACE of PENTACLES

Season: None

Description: A large hand holding a pentacle has emerged from a cloud in a clear, blue sky. A well-tended garden is below.

The Ace of Pentacles signifies new beginnings. Everything is going your way. Your health is likely to be good, and there are positive financial opportunities opening up. This is a good time to start anything involving money and business. This card symbolizes opportunity, attainment, ultimate prosperity, abundance, health and worthwhile goals. This is a good time to start anything that has the potential to make money.

Reversed: This is a sign of frustration, delays, and uncertainty concerning money matters. You need to make sure that your goals are worthwhile ones, and that you're prepared to do whatever it takes to make them happen. If your goals aren't what you really want to achieve, take time out to work out what it is you really want to do, and then set new goals for yourself.

2 of PENTACLES

Season: Winter

Description: A young man danc-
es on the outskirts of a town with a
pentacle in each hand. The pentacles are joined by a cord creating an
infinity sign. This shows that he can
handle almost anything. Although
he has a serious expression on his
face, the young man is obviously
enjoying dancing.

The Two of Pentacles indicates
the need to balance every aspect
of your life. You need to remain
calm and flexible. The young man
in the card illustrates this, as his
expression is calm, even though he
is juggling the two pentacles. If you
can maintain balance and harmony in your life at this time, your financial
situation will slowly improve, even though you may feel stretched at times.

This card symbolizes balance, changes, harmony, adjustment,
multi-tasking and steady progress.

Reversed: This is a time to be cautious with money. You probably feel
as if you have too many obligations. Avoid extravagance, and question
whether or not you really need to buy non essential items now. Money is
likely to be tight, but this situation won't last for long.

3 of PENTACLES

Season: Late Winter and Early Spring

Description: A priest and a monk watch a sculptor carving a figure in a church. They are directing the process, though the sculptor is the one doing the actual work.

The Three of Pentacles indicates the need to work well within a group to achieve a worthwhile goal. You may not receive all the recognition or financial reward that you deserve for your hard work. As the goal has not yet been achieved, you'll need patience, endurance, and be prepared to accept that you still have much to learn.

The Three of Pentacles represents teamwork, creativity, skill, appreciation, knowledge, learning, quality, recognition, advancement, promotion, increased status, and a worthwhile challenge.

Reversed: You need to work hard to get along with others at this time. Act responsibly and do your share of the work. You'll experience problems if you take shortcuts, or are too casual about what you're supposed to be doing. You may need to develop new skills, or work harder, to impress your superiors.

4 of PENTACLES

Season: Spring

Description: A man wearing a crown is sitting with his feet on two pentacles. He is firmly holding a pentacle in his hands, and a fourth pentacle sits on top of his crown. In addition, he has a closed sack, presumably full of money, beside him. He is grimly hanging on to what he has.

The Four of Pentacles indicates financial security, but there's also a fear of letting go of what you already have. It indicates a degree of success, but can also indicate that you're scared to take a chance, and because of this, risk becoming stuck where you are. You may need to learn to delegate, and not try to do everything yourself.

This card symbolizes possessiveness, jealousy, control, hanging on, maintaining the status quo, materialism and lack of trust.

Reversed: If you're greedy, and strive after money and possessions at this time, you'll suffer as a result. You'll need to be fair, honest, and easy to get along with to make the most of this period.

5 of PENTACLES

Season: Late Spring and Early Summer

Description: It's a snowy night and two travellers, cold, hungry and destitute, walk past a house with a lit window containing five pentacles. It's possible that this window is the stained glass window of a church. The travellers are in the dark, even though there is comfort and light just a few feet away.

The Five of Pentacles is a card of lack and rejection. The people in the card are lacking the basic necessities of life, and are suffering from ill health, lack of money and shelter. The lack is likely to be financial, but may also relate to health and a lack of support.

This card symbolizes poverty, lack, destitution, deprivation, despair, rejection, health concerns and an inability to look ahead. You may feel lonely and insecure, no matter what the real situation happens to be. Minimize your outgoings, and start thinking more positively about the future.

Reversed: A problem that has been concerning you for some time will gradually be resolved. Live within your means, and don't take advantage of other people's kindness and generosity. Everything is gradually improving for you, but it will take a while for you to realize this.

6 of PENTACLES

Season: Summer

Description: An obviously well-to-do man holds a pair of scales in his right hand and passes out money to a woman with his left. A man holds his hands out in the hope of receiving money, too. The scales the man carries symbolize fairness and justice. Six pentacles float in the air around the benefactor.

The Six of Pentacles represents kindness and generosity. You might be the person who is being generous, or you may receive financial aid from someone else. Consequently, this card means both to give and to receive.

This card symbolizes generosity, sharing, charity, donations, loans, philanthropy, gratitude, appreciation, and sharing with others. It's a good time to do some voluntary work, and to help people who are less fortunate than you. As it works both ways, the Six of Pentacles also symbolizes asking for help.

Reversed: This is the time when you receive payback for what you've done in the past. This can be positive or negative, depending on your past actions. If you're done good things for others, you'll receive all the help you need. If you've been stingy and miserly, you may find it hard to get much sympathy or help from others.

7 of PENTACLES

Season: Late Summer and Early Autumn

Description: A man is having a break from his work to gaze at seven pentacles that are attached to a bush. He is willing to wait for his hard work to bear fruit.

The Seven of Pentacles indicates the stage where all the hard work has been done, and now there is a pause before it starts to pay off. It indicates you have adopted a long-term view, and are prepared to work hard and wait patiently for the rewards of your labour. This is a good time to think about future goals and what you'd like to achieve next. Your finances are starting to improve as a result of the work you have put in.

This card symbolizes assessment, reflection, rewards from effort, success, patience, possible delays and slow but steady progress.

Reversed: This is a sign of disappointment and disillusionment, as something hasn't gone according to plan, or has failed to work out. Don't give up as you're close to success. There are likely to be money concerns at this time. Pause, re-evaluate the situation, make new plans, and then start moving forward again.

8 of PENTACLES

Season: Autumn

Description: An artisan is busy at his work. The eight pentacles show that he is receiving financial rewards from his efforts.

The Eight of Pentacles shows that you already possess, or can learn, the necessary skills to achieve your goals. You're willing to focus on the task at hand and stay with it until it is completed. You're gaining great pleasure and satisfaction from your work. You are already reaping some of the rewards of success, but much more is to come as long as you're disciplined and work hard.

This card symbolizes work, skill, diligence, determination, enthusiasm, apprenticeship, craftsmanship, application, knowledge, financial security, investments, attention to detail and learning.

Reversed: This is a sign of discouragement at your apparent lack of success. You might be tempted to take shortcuts, or feel angry and impatient. Ask people you trust for help and advice. Take a day or two off to replenish your soul, and think things through. You'll feel happier and more confident when you return to your work.

9 of PENTACLES

Season: Late Autumn and Early Winter

Description: A woman stands in a vineyard with a bird on her hand. The grapes are abundant and are ready to harvest. Nine pentacles are attached to the vines, and in front of her is a small snail. The snail shows that even though everything looks perfect in the scene, in reality, nothing is perfect. Snails also symbolize slow, but steady, progress.

The Nine of Pentacles indicates wealth and prosperity that has been obtained through dedication and hard work. There are feelings of peace, gratification and satisfaction.

This card symbolizes achievement, material satisfaction, wealth, completion, self-worth, pleasure, property, enjoying the best life has to offer, and time on your own.

Reversed: You may feel that all your efforts have provided little in the way of financial reward. Be patient, as good times are not far away. You may be seeking recognition or praise from someone else. This won't be forthcoming, and you'll have to be satisfied knowing that you've done the best you can. Be careful of anything that sounds too good to be true.

10 of PENTACLES

Season: All

Description: An older man sits in his garden, surrounded by his family and dogs. The large house visible through the archway indicates his wealth, as do the ten pentacles superimposed over the scene.

The Ten of Pentacles is the card of material success. It shows that you're creating a good solid, comfortable foundation for your family. This could indicate the purchase of a house, or anything else that can provide stability and the potential for future growth. This is a conservative card, showing a conventional family enjoying the good life. Share your good fortune with others.

This card symbolizes family, friendship, foundation, continuity, values, wealth, investment, accomplishment, inheritance, reputation and tradition.

Reversed: Remember there's much more to life than money and possessions. Think about what's really important to you. Spend time with the people you love, and tell them how much they mean to you. In your quiet times, think about the spiritual, nonmaterial, side of life. Don't take any unnecessary risks at this time.

—⁓—

SUIT OF WANDS

The Suit of Wands relates to the element of Fire. It relates to the suit of clubs in a regular deck of playing cards. Fire is a masculine element. It is enthusiastic, passionate, creative, volatile and transformative. Fire needs to be controlled as it can be both positive and negative. The warming Sun is positive as it brings life, but lightning gives a clue as to how destructive this element can become. The Wands relate to the Fire signs of Aries, Leo and Sagittarius.

ACE of WANDS

Season: None

Description: A hand holding a flowering wand emerges from a cloud. Below is a hilly landscape and a small castle.

The Ace of Wands is a sign of a significant burst of creative energy. You will be full of ideas and feel inspired, optimistic, enthusiastic, energetic, excited, and ready to make a bold leap forward. This card denotes an opportunity that holds great promise, but at this stage it is more like an acorn, than an oak tree.

This card symbolizes inspiration, energy, creativity, potential, beginnings, confidence, enthusiasm, adventure and courage.

Reversed: You're likely to feel frustrated and dissatisfied with your lack of progress. Something either failed to get started, or may not have had enough energy to keep going. Some of your problems are out of your control, and there's nothing you can do except wait until the situation becomes easier. While you're waiting, look at your own attitudes and behaviour to see if they could be holding you back. Once you start, nothing will be able to hold you back.

2 of WANDS

Season: Winter

Description: A successful man looks out to sea. He holds a staff in his right hand and a globe in the other. Another staff is to his left. Attached to the battlements is a coat of arms showing crossed roses and lilies.

The Two of Wands is the card of opportunity. It shows that different ideas have been implemented, but there is still a great deal to do. The globe shows that the man has at least one plan underway. The fact that he's holding a staff (wand) indicates that he has other ideas in reserve, just in case they're necessary. His unusual headwear shows that he's independent, and is not concerned about what other people think. He feels powerful and in control.

This card symbolizes authority, power, energy, creativity, originality, vision, goal-setting, boldness, personal power, forward progress and decision making.

Reversed: You're likely to be feeling uncertain and insecure, as despite all your efforts, nothing seems to be happening. Don't allow the discouragement of others to hold you back. Look at your plans again, and take one small step forward. Others will follow.

3 of WANDS

Season: Late Winter and Early Spring

Description: A man stands gazing out to sea. Beside him are three staffs (wands) standing upright in the ground. He grasps one with his left hand. From this vantage point he is able to see the whole picture.

The Three of Wands is a sign of satisfaction. Something important has been achieved, and the man gazing out to sea knows that more success will follow. This card shows that there are opportunities for expansion and growth, but time is required for the results to become apparent. There is the possibility of travel at this time.

This card symbolizes hope, optimism, expectations, vision, foresight, leadership, expansion, opportunities and potential.

Reversed: You may feel you're working twice as hard as you should be, and are still making little progress. You're feeling disappointed and downhearted. Think carefully before making any important decisions, as your judgment may not be as good as it usually is. Take time out for rest and relaxation.

4 of WANDS

Season: Spring

Description: A garland is hanging from four flowering wands. Beneath it, two young women are making bouquets of flowers, possibly for a celebration of some sort.

The Four of Wands indicates a time to rest and relax after a period of hard work. The work has proved worthwhile and the rewards are starting to be realized, making this a card of peace and contentment. This card can indicate a celebration, possibly a birthday, wedding, family occasion, or a rite of passage. It may be a celebration to mark the successful conclusion of a project.

This card symbolizes celebration, contentment, home, peace, harmony, excitement, prosperity and family.

Reversed: Despite being reversed, this is still a positive card. This is a sign of modest success. You might feel slightly disappointed as you'd expected more, but at least you're moving in the right direction. Everything you do takes longer than you think, or is harder than you expected. Be persistent and clearly focused on what you want. Avoid negative people, and allow time to celebrate.

5 of WANDS

Season: Late Spring and Early Summer

Description: Five young men are brandishing wands in what appears to be a light-hearted fight.

The Five of Wands indicates a time of delays and frustrations. Nothing goes your way. You'll experience plenty of minor setbacks and irritations, but none of them last for long. The five men appear to be engaged in child's play, as no one is getting hurt, and all the wands make contact with other wands, rather than people. This can be fun, but no progress is being made. When this card appears, it's usually a sign of wasted time and energy. You may be trying to do too many different things at the same time. If this is the case, you need to make sure you're spending your time wisely. This card can also indicate competition and rivalry.

This card symbolizes physical activities, competition, conflict, strife, play, assertiveness, obstacles, disagreements, tension and wasting time.

Reversed: This is a sign that other people could be trying to undermine you. Even though they're likely to lie and cheat, you need to remain scrupulously honest, as you know that right will ultimately win. Once you've won this battle, you'll start moving ahead again.

6 of WANDS

Season: Summer

Description: A horseman is carrying a wand with a laurel wreath, the sign of victory, attached to it. Five flowering wands are being carried by other people.

The Six of Wands indicates success and recognition by others. This could be a promotion, a pay increase, or even public recognition. It is a sign of victory, and other people are congratulating you on your achievements.

This card symbolizes victory, success, recognition, honour, pride, acknowledgment, advancement, achievement, self-confidence and pride.

Reversed: You may feel ignored and rejected by others. Remember that this is only temporary. Put your time to good use and be prepared to wait until the situation improves. There's likely to be a misunderstanding caused by lack of proper communication.

7 of WANDS

Season: Late Summer and Early Autumn

Description: A man wearing a suit of armour holds a flowering wand in a position to defend himself. Six more flowering wands appear to oppose his progress. The man knows he's in a powerful position as he appears unconcerned and stands uphill from his possible attackers.

The Seven of Wands shows that you're standing up for yourself and possibly looking for support to help you achieve your goals. Other people are opposing your rightful position and you are being forced to defend yourself. You need to use courage and persistence to defend your position against your competitors, but you have the necessary qualities to do this and know you will triumph in the end. Remain firm in your convictions. You need to be resolute and go after what you want. There is no need to compromise or give in.

This card symbolizes challenge, competition, determination, courage, integrity, strength of character, assertiveness, standing up for yourself and taking a stand.

Reversed: You need to stand up for yourself, but make sure you don't overreact. Speak your mind and try not to feel hurt by the comments of others. Let other people know where you stand, and refuse to compromise your principles. Continue working towards your goals.

8 of WANDS

Season: Autumn

Description: A flight of flowering wands is heading downwards towards the ground. In the background is a river and a castle. As there are no figures in this card, the wands indicate a number of possibilities falling into place. Everything is going your way.

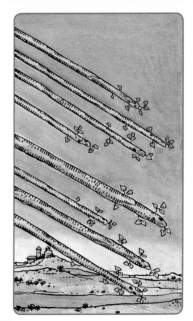

The Eight of Wands denotes an exciting time with many opportunities to explore. You'll be happy, yet busy, as there's a great deal of activity going on. If you remain focussed on your goals you'll progress quickly.

This card symbolizes speed, action, energy, movement, travel, versatility, enthusiasm, information, and acting quickly and decisively.

Reversed: You're likely to feel that you're swimming against the tide, and are experiencing more than your share of delays and frustrations. Instead of fighting against these, slow down, and stop wasting time and energy. Take time out and see if you can find a different path for yourself.

9 of WANDS

Season: Late Autumn and Early Winter

Description: A man leans upon his staff. Behind him eight staffs are lined up in a row. They appear to be protecting him.

The Nine of Wands indicates that you are struggling against outside pressures. You are close to success, but now you have a final challenge to overcome. Fortunately, this card indicates persistence, and you have the necessary determination and stamina to withstand these difficulties. You need to stand up for yourself, and demonstrate what you believe in.

This card symbolizes hope, encouragement, resilience, loyalty, strength, discipline, stamina, hidden reserves, and the ability to keep moving forward despite difficulties.

Reversed: You're likely to feel disillusioned as something or someone you used to believe in has shown their true colours. Let go. There's no point fighting for a cause you no longer believe in. Learn from the experience, and start anew.

10 of WANDS

Season: All

Description: A man is slowly making his way home. He's carrying a heavy burden of ten flowering wands, and is struggling to carry them all even though he knows he's almost home.

The Ten of Wands is a sign that you've taken on too many responsibilities and concerns, and are suffering under their weight. You're probably over-worked and over-tired. This card is a sign that you should delegate or let go of some of the burden you're carrying. Let other people help you and take some of the load. Do not neglect physical fitness and exercise, as overwork can lead to health problems.

This card symbolizes burdens, responsibilities, obligations, duty, stress, pressure, hard work and trying to do too much.

Reversed: You're likely to feel exhausted by all the hard work you've put in. However, you've almost reached your goal, and the heavy load you're carrying will soon be lifted. You need to persist a little bit longer to achieve the rewards you deserve. It will soon be time to relax and enjoy happy times with family and friends.

—⟋⟍—

SUIT OF SWORDS

The Suit of Swords relates to the element of Air. Air is the intellectual element and enjoys thinking, communicating and socializing, Air enjoys interacting with other people and needs plenty of stimulating ideas to think about and discuss. In a regular deck of playing cards this element is represented by the suit of spades. The Swords relate to the Air signs of Gemini, Libra and Aquarius.

ACE of SWORDS

Season: None

Description: A hand clutching a sword emerges from a cloud. A crown, symbolizing mental clarity, hovers over the tip of the sword, and fronds of olive and laurel hang down from it.

The Ace of Swords indicates a new beginning, one which offers great strength and power. The sword is double-edged and gives you the necessary power to cut through anything that could impede your progress. The risk is that excessive force could be applied. You must use your skills and talents positively. The Ace of Swords also provides you with mental clarity that enables you to come up with excellent ideas and see through any potential difficulties that could occur as you move forward again.

This card symbolizes intellect, truth, reason, victory, power, force, energy, action, communication and knowledge.

Reversed: Someone, possibly you, is using his or her personal power to control and dominate others. You'll need to modify your behaviour if it's you. If it's someone else refuse to let them manipulate and use you. There is often a loss of some sort when this card is reversed.

2 of SWORDS

Season: Winter

Description: A blindfolded woman holds two upright swords. She is sitting on a chair with her back to the sea. Above her, a crescent Moon adds light to the picture.

The Two of Swords shows you're trying to avoid making a choice or decision. At the moment you are stuck, and a change needs to be made to allow you to move forward again. The blindfold shows that you don't want to see what needs to be seen. The Moon relates to your intuition. Its presence indicates that you're using your intellect, but are refusing to listen to the small, quiet voice inside you. Your emotions are likely to be hard to control at this time.

This card symbolizes stalemate, indecision, need for give and take, stubbornness, denial, avoidance and a temporary pause.

Reversed: You're likely to find it hard to make an important decision, as you're trying to make it using reason alone. Listen to what others have to say, and let them know exactly how you feel. Listen to what your strong emotions are trying to tell you. Take whatever time you need to make your mind up, and then act.

3 of SWORDS

Season: Late Winter and Early Spring

Description: A man is lying on the ground with his hands clasped to his face. Above him is a heart pierced by three swords. The clouds are heavy and it's raining in the distance.

The Three of Swords is a sign of arguments, disagreements, and emotional suffering in your relationships. You need to cut away anything that has outworn its use to make room for new growth. Although this card usually means that you're the one receiving pain, it's also possible that you might be inflicting pain on others.

This card symbolizes heartbreak, sorrow, sadness, grief, disloyalty, rejection, betrayal, separation, loneliness and sudden, unexpected pain.

Reversed: You're likely to feel confused, anxious and hurt, as people you trusted have let you down, or could be talking about you behind your back. Don't waste time dwelling on this. Tell them what you think of their callous behaviour, and move on. The difficulties are finally behind you, and although the pain may stay with you for a while, your situation is steadily improving.

4 of SWORDS

Season: Spring

Description: A knight in armour is lying on a bed with his hands raised in prayer. Three swords, pointing downwards, are hanging on the wall behind him. A fourth sword is resting diagonally, crossing his body. It's possible that he's resting on a tomb, as behind him is a stained glass window indicating that he may be inside a church.

The Four of Swords indicates a time to rest and recuperate after a period of stress and difficulty. It could indicate a period of time to recover from an illness. You should make the most of this enforced vacation, as shortly you will return to your normal, everyday life with all of its challenges and complications. Meditate, think matters through, and enjoy feeling peaceful and calm.

This card symbolizes contemplation, meditation, recuperation, rest, preparation, relaxation, thinking, and listening to your inner voice.

Reversed: You have enjoyed taking some time out, but now it's time to return to your everyday life. You'll be kept busy, and experiencing a great deal of stress and pressure. Don't accept more work than you can handle. Keep a positive outlook, and remind yourself that better times are ahead.

5 of SWORDS

Season: Late Spring and Early Summer

Description: A man in armour stands on a beach looking back at two men who are walking away from him. Their body language shows dejection and defeat, and their two swords lie on the sand. The man in armour holds two swords over his left shoulder. They both point upward. In his right hand he holds a sword pointing downward to the sand. Dark clouds are appearing in the sky. Although there has been a disagreement, no one has been physically hurt, showing that this was largely a battle of words.

The Five of Swords indicates a conflict or disagreement. At this stage, you may think you've won, but this may not be the case as you've hurt or angered other people, and you may feel isolated and lonely. You'll likely to wonder if the apparent victory was worth it. You may need to come to a compromise to restore your reputation and move ahead again.

This card symbolizes victory, assertion, self-interest, hostility, betrayal, deceit, revenge, obstacles that need to be overcome carefully, and looking out for number one.

Reversed: You may feel as if you've won a victory, but in reality, your losses are just as great, or even greater, than those of your opponent. Be careful who you trust and confide in, as your opponents will do all they can to defeat you.

6 of SWORDS

Season: Summer

Description: A ferryman is taking a figure with a covered head across a river. Six swords are thrust into the boat's timbers and surround the right side of this mysterious figure. The water is smooth and the sky is gray, but not threatening. The boat is getting close to land on the far side of the river.

The Six of Swords shows that you're moving away from your difficulties. You feel regretful about the situation, and the need to let go of something. The release of tension accompanying this decision creates feelings of calm and hope for the future. You instinctively know that the future will be much better than the past.

This card symbolizes travel, escape, leaving problems behind, journey over water, loss, struggle, sadness and recovery.

Reversed: This indicates frustrations, delays, and unforeseen difficulties. You're likely to feel hemmed in and limited in what you can do to resolve the situation. Stand up for what you believe in, and look for opportunities to start moving forward again.

7 of SWORDS

Season: Late Summer and Early Autumn

Description: This is sometimes known as "the thief" card as it shows someone sneaking away from a military camp with five swords in his arms. Two more swords remain stuck in the ground.

The Seven of Swords is a card of betrayal and deception. It's a sign of caution if you're tempted to do something secret or underhand, as you'll be caught out if you do. It can also mean avoiding your obligations, hiding from the truth, and avoiding responsibility. You also need to be cautious that you don't become a victim of the duplicity of someone else.

This card symbolizes betrayal, deception, cunning, dishonesty, stealth, sabotage, manipulation, escape, and covering your tracks.

Reversed: If you act honestly and honourably, you'll get through this difficult stage with an increased reputation. If you try anything sneaky or underhand, you're likely to be caught out. Work on your long term goals while you're waiting for the situation to become clearer.

8 of SWORDS

Season: Autumn

Description: A blindfolded woman is bound to a tree. Surrounding her are eight swords with their tips embedded in the ground. However, it looks as if the blindfold and bindings could be released easily, indicating that the difficult position this woman finds herself within could be self-imposed.

The Eight of Swords indicates that you feel trapped and confined by your own thoughts and fears. The symbolic blindfold might have been put on you by others, but only you can remove it. You might be your own worst enemy now. You need to gain a new perspective, and this different point of view will show you the way forward. There will be a number of choices, and you'll need to evaluate them carefully before deciding which one to choose. You have the power to free yourself and move forward.

This card symbolizes isolation, confinement, indecision, powerlessness, bondage, restriction, loss of control, limited, trapped, confusion and lack of confidence.

Reversed: Your main concerns are behind you now, and you can start progressing again. However, because of what you've been through, you may find it hard to trust others, and could be dwelling on insignificant problems rather than looking ahead.

9 of SWORDS

Season: Late Autumn and Early Winter

Description: A woman lies in bed with nine swords hanging over her. She has woken up from a nightmare and is unable to fall sleep again. She holds her hands to her eyes as she tries to relax enough to drift off into sleep. This card is commonly referred to as the "nightmare" card.

The Nine of Swords indicates that your problems are being caused by your own thoughts. You are worrying too much. These worries often relate to fears about the future. You are being overly hard on yourself, and blame yourself for everything that has gone wrong. You need to take control of your thoughts, be kind to yourself, and eliminate as many negative thoughts as you can.

This card symbolizes anxiety, despair, depression, fear, uncertainty, guilt, frustration, sleeplessness, nightmares, stress, loss, anguish and worry.

Reversed: The situation is improving by the day, but you may not be aware of this as you're still suffering from stress and worry. Take control of your imagination, and think of all the good things in your life. You are finally on track again.

10 of SWORDS

Season: All

Description: A man is lying on his back with ten swords plunged into him. The sky is black and ominous.

The Ten of Spades indicates a sudden defeat, setback, loss or ending. This could be a misfortune that simply occurs without reason. Alternatively, someone might have been stabbing you in the back and engineering your downfall. The lesson of this card is to accept the situation. You need to get up, learn from the experience, and start again. The pain and anguish may seem hard to bear, but you will learn from this experience, and become a much stronger person as a result. You will have a better outlook on life in the future, too.

This card symbolizes failure, defeat, betrayal, loss, pain, disaster, ruin, misfortune, self-pity, clarity, endings and new starts.

Reversed: You might be in a state of denial about your current situation. Accept the fact that you've reached a turning point, and an old cycle has come to an end. Spend time with family and friends, and restore your energy and zest for life. Once you can accept that what's happened has happened, you can let go of the past and start again.

COURT CARDS

The Court cards are the most difficult cards in the deck to interpret. This is because they can be interpreted in a number of different ways. Traditionally, they were interpreted as people, but nowadays they're often considered to be symbols, forms of energy, or an aspect of the personality of the person having the reading.

COURT CARDS AS PEOPLE

Let's start by looking at the Court cards as the people we interact with. Sometimes it's obvious who the person is, but at other times you'll have to think about the characteristics of the person depicted on the card to work out who it might be. To compound the situation, these cards can also represent aspects of yourself. Fortunately, with practice, you'll instantly know if the card depicts you or someone else. In addition to this, the cards do not necessarily denote the correct gender of the person. Usually, a king or a knight will be male, but this is not necessarily the case. In fact, it's possible for the husband in a marriage to be represented by a queen, while his wife is depicted by the king. This is because he's expressing attributes usually associated with a queen, and his wife expressing the attributes of a king.

At times, the Court cards can indicate a situation or happening that has a personality of its own. The Knave of Chalices, for instance, might indicate an invitation to a happy occasion, rather than a specific person.

Many people will be involved in your question if a number of Court cards appear in the spread.

As the Court cards can be confusing, we'll start by looking at each card as a group. There are four of these: the Kings, Queens, Knights and Knaves.

- **THE KINGS**

The kings are charismatic, and possess authority and power. They make important decisions, and are regularly consulted for advice and counsel. They are confident, responsible, experienced, worldly and wise. They are usually older people, and are considered the father figure in the family of the suit they belong to. They prefer the overall picture, and prefer not to involve themselves in details.

- **THE QUEENS**

The Queens are caring, nurturing, passionate and loving. They are confident, experienced, powerful, and enjoy sharing their knowledge and expertise. They are usually subtle, and achieve their aims using tact, diplomacy and femininity. They are controlled and possess emotional strength. They remain composed in every type of situation. The queens are usually older women who are the mother figure in the family of the suit they belong to.

- **THE KNIGHTS**

The Knights and the Pages indicate the children of the King and Queen. The Knights are older and more mature. Usually, they are already pursuing a career, and possess drive and ambition. These are good qualities, but because they don't yet have the wisdom and maturity of the Kings and Queens, they sometimes race into a situation without thinking the matter through first. The Knights denote fast, decisive action. They also carry messages and defend the kingdom.

- **THE KNAVES**

The Knaves are the youngest members of the court, and represent the future. At this stage, they have no power, but will already be showing promise for the future. As the Knaves are young, they bring a youthful, even playful, element into your life. However, they may need to be watched to keep them on track. The Knaves can also indicate an older person who is young at heart, The Knaves are energetic, excitable, enthusiastic, and keen to learn. They indicate beginnings, renewal, change and transformation.

A DIFFERENT APPROACH

Sometimes the Court cards have symbolic meanings, and don't relate to a specific person. A knave, for instance, might indicate a message or an invitation, a knight could indicate travel or movement, a queen might symbolize creating or nurturing something, and a king could indicate managing or directing some activity.

The cards might indicate someone's level of emotional maturity. The presence of a knave, for instance, could indicate that the person asking the question is behaving in an immature manner, no matter how young or old he or she might be.

A knave might indicate the early stages of a project, while a king could signify completion.

The Court cards can also represent aspects of the personality of the person having the reading. It can be an interesting exercise to look at all the Court cards in your deck and see what aspects of each card relate to you.

Another way of looking at the Court cards is to consider them as energies, rather than as people. Consequently, the Knight of Pentacles is energy that's being used to move forward financially. The Queen of Chalices is energy that's expressing love, compassion and intuition. These can be energies you (or the person you're reading for) already possess, or need to develop, to help resolve the current situation.

The hardest part is knowing which of the various possibilities apply in the particular reading you're doing. There is no need to worry about this. Start by looking at the Court cards as people, and then experiment with other possibilities as you gain experience. In time, your intuition will tell you which possibility to use at any given time.

THE CHALICES FAMILY

The Suit of Chalices belongs to the element of Water, and this relates to feelings, emotions, compassion, empathy and intuition.

KNAVE of CHALICES

Description: A young man is standing outdoors on the sand. There are mountains in the background. He watches a fish emerge from the cup he is holding in his right hand. This fish appears to speak to him. The fish symbolizes

creativity, emotions, imagination and intuition, and is a sign that the young man can harness them and make them real.

The Knave of Chalices indicates a young man or woman who is creative, imaginative and curious about life. He or she is likely to be sensitive and easily hurt. It can also indicate the start of a creative project, and the person should listen to the messages that come from his or her subconscious mind.

This card symbolizes someone who is naïve, dreamy, immature, gullible, youthful, misunderstood, agreeable, affectionate, loving, intuitive and sensitive. It also symbolizes creativity, emotions, intuition, important family events, and new projects.

Reversed: You may suffer from procrastination and lack of motivation. You are failing to meet other people's expectations. There are a number of minor problems that need to be dealt with. Resolve one of these at a time. Your success in dealing with these will improve your attitude and make it easier to move ahead.

KNIGHT of CHALICES

Description: It's a beautiful day and a knight rides his white horse slowly alongside a river and a waterfall. He holds a cup in his right hand. The scene is calm, and the young knight appears to be delivering a message, rather than riding to or from battle.

The Knight of Chalices denotes a young man who is attractive and gets on well with others. He is in touch with his feelings, and invariably follows whatever his heart tells him to do. When this card appears in a spread it's usually a sign of an invitation or message. Unlike the Page of Chalices, who is still seeking a purpose, the Knight has already started on a journey that involves his intuition, creativity and desire for action. As knights always act speedily, you can expect changes to occur.

This card symbolizes love, romance, charm, new experiences, refinement, intuition, compassion and sensitivity. The Knight of Chalices relates to the astrological sign of Pisces.

Reversed: Don't accept anything at face value. Ask questions, research, and talk with others before making your mind up. Be realistic about potential rewards, as nothing worthwhile happens without considerable hard work and effort.

QUEEN of CHALICES

Description: A queen is shown sitting on a green throne surrounded by water. She is gazing at a cup she's holding in her right hand.

The Queen of Chalices denotes a mature woman who is family-minded, honest and warm-hearted. She uses her sensitivity, empathy and intuition to help others. She uses her heart more than her head, and because of this may be highly creative as well as compassionate. She certainly appreciate beauty in all its forms. When this card appears it's a sign that you should get more in touch with your feelings and intuition.

This card symbolizes emotional security, intuition, compassion, empathy, sensitivity, calmness, creativity, spirituality and love. The Queen of Chalices relates to the astrological sign of Scorpio.

Reversed: A strong woman may not be as honest or as honourable as you think. Think before acting, and don't believe everything you hear. There is the possibility of deceit, gossip, and people talking behind your back. Trust your intuition.

KING of CHALICES

Description: A king is shown sitting on a large green throne that is riding on the sea. He holds a sceptre in his left hand and a cup in his right. Behind him, to his left, is a sailing ship. Behind him, on his right, a dolphin leaps out of the water. The sea depicts the Water element and relates to the subconscious mind. The dolphin and the ship show that the king is aware of his emotions, feelings and intuitions, and handles them in a mature, responsible manner.

The King of Chalices denotes someone who successfully balances his emotions and intellect. He is emotionally mature, and acts calmly and responsibly. This can indicate an older man who is family-minded, and appears to be gentle, kind, caring, cultured and generous. He is likely to be successful in his career, and can cooperate and get along well with everyone.

This card symbolizes compassion, understanding, sensitivity, consideration, diplomacy and responsibility. The King of Chalices relates to the astrological sign of Cancer.

Reversed: This is a sign of dishonesty. An egotistical man may appear charming at first, and will impress you with his apparent skills and connections. However, he has an ulterior motive, and will try to use you for his own ends.

THE PENTACLES FAMILY

The suit of Pentacles belongs to the element of Earth, and this relates to the material world: finances, property, possessions, and worldly pleasures.

KNAVE of PENTACLES

Description: A young person is standing in a rural setting gazing at a large pentacle that he or she is holding. This is person appears to be dreaming about the possible riches that lie ahead.

The Knave of Pentacles, like all the other knave cards, signifies new beginnings and positive opportunities. The person represented by the card is aware of these possibilities, and is starting to make plans and deciding how to turn these ideas to his or her advantage. You will probably need to learn new skills. You will have to keep your feet on the ground and be realistic about the possible risks and rewards.

This card symbolizes expansion, future success, ambition, drive, opportunities, determination and persistence.

Reversed: Money that is expected fails to materialize, leading to a temporary shortage. You'll be disappointed and feel disillusioned. Keep a tight rein on your finances until this problem is resolved.

KNIGHT of PENTACLES

Description: A knight in full armour sits on his black horse and gazes into the distance. He holds a pentacle in his right hand, but appears to be more interested in what lies further ahead.

The Knight of Pentacles has experienced the dreams of the Page of Pentacles, and is now clearly focussed on attaining his or her goals. This is a card of hard work, but with the promise of reward. The tasks may seem tedious, even boring at times, but the necessary groundwork needs to be done properly to ensure ultimate success. This card indicates slow, but steady, progress.

This card symbolizes efficiency, routine, responsibility, reliability, honesty, stability, caution, realistic goals and hard work. The Knight of Pentacles relates to the astrological sign of Virgo.

Reversed: You'll disappoint both yourself and others by your lack of motivation at this time. You might need to force yourself to act responsibly and fulfil your obligations. Laziness and lethargy are bad habits to fall into, and your reputation will suffer if you don't regain your enthusiasm and energy.

QUEEN of PENTACLES

Description: A queen is sitting on her throne in a garden surrounded by flowers, symbolizing abundance. She is holding a pentacle with both hands.

The Queen of Pentacles signifies a mature, motherly woman who has a down-to-earth, practical approach to life. She enjoys nurturing and caring for others, and making sure their material needs are attended to. She has prospered as a result of her hard work, and is now more concerned with looking after the people who are close to her. This card relates to caring for others, or being cared for by others. It also relates to financial success.

This card symbolizes nurture, abundance, prosperity, loyalty, care for others, warm-hearted, generosity, love, honesty and resourcefulness. The Queen of Pentacles relates to the astrological sign of Taurus.

Reversed: You may feel a loss of confidence. Refuse to allow yourself to become a victim of other people's idle comments. A discontented, unhappy woman may be causing problems. Nurture yourself, avoid negative people, and continue working towards your own goals.

KING of PENTACLES

Description: An obviously prosperous king is sitting on a throne outside his castle. He holds a sceptre in his right hand and a pentacle in his left. The sceptre symbolizes power, and the pentacle symbolizes his financial authority. Plants are growing over and around his throne, signifying abundance and growth.

The King of Pentacles signifies ambition, power, leadership, worldly success, and attainment on a large scale. He has devoted his life to worldly success, and now enjoys giving advice and guidance to others to enable them to prosper, too. He is a mature, pragmatic, fatherly man who enjoys all the good things life has to offer.

This card symbolizes ambition, status, material satisfaction, practicality, philanthropy, opportunity, reliability, honesty and appreciation. The King of Pentacles relates to the astrological sign of Capricorn.

Reversed: Avoid any opportunities that seem too good to be true. A gambler, speculator or conman could give you a tip that sounds feasible, but isn't. Think carefully before acting, and don't invest in anything without taking professional advice.

THE WANDS FAMILY

The suit of Wands belongs to the element of Fire, and this relates to vitality, energy, passion and creation.

KNAVE of WANDS

Description: A young man stands on a plateau in the mountains and gazes upward. He is thinking about his dreams and goals. He holds a flowering staff with both hands.

The Knave of Wands, like the other knaves, represents change and new opportunities. He or she is young, and because of this, may be ignored or not listened to. As the knave belongs to the Fire element, he'll be passionate and possess a strong zest for life. This card can indicate a creative idea that can be nurtured and developed into something worthwhile. You have the necessary drive and enthusiasm to take this a long way. The Knave of Wands can also indicate a messenger who brings you exciting and positive news. It can also indicate someone who wants to help you see your life in a totally different way.

This card symbolizes enthusiasm, creativity, courage, self-belief, optimism, assertion, energy, passion and a strong desire to be involved in what is going on.

Reversed: Some unexpected bad news causes problems. See what you could have done to have prevented them, learn from the experience, and move on.

KNIGHT of WANDS

Description: A knight in full armour is setting out on a journey. He holds a flowering staff in his right hand. He is riding through a desert and three pyramids can be seen behind him.

The Knave of Knights came up with an idea, and the Knight of Wands is following it through with great enthusiasm and energy. He is inclined to be reckless, impatient and overly assertive, and these traits can hold him back until he learns how to control them. This knight can sometimes indicate a love relationship with someone much older or younger than you. A major change is about to occur, and this will provide you with many new and stimulating possibilities to pursue.

This card symbolizes action, impulsiveness, adventure, speed, loyalty, confidence, travel and new experiences. The Knight of Wands relates to the astrological sign of Sagittarius.

Reversed: This is a time of frustrations and confusion. Do your best to keep calm, even when people deliberately antagonize you. You'll make the problem considerably worse if you lash out in anger or frustration. Pay special attention to your close relationships, and don't let small things bother or concern you.

QUEEN of WANDS

Description: A queen is sitting outdoors on a golden throne that contains the heads of two lions facing opposite directions. This signifies strength and fire. The queen holds a large flowering staff in her right hand and a sunflower in her left. Sunflowers are a symbol of fertility and fruitfulness. Sitting in front of her throne is a black cat, symbolizing the occult, or hidden side, of the Queen of Wands.

The Queen of Wands is independent, strong, and fully able to stand up for herself. She is enthusiastic and energetic, two qualities she needs, as she leads a busy, active life. She is extroverted, outgoing, sociable, and a good conversationalist. Despite having strong opinions, she makes friends easily. She is creative in both thought and deed. She sets high standards for herself and others, and sticks to her goals until she's achieve them. She's happy to provide expert advice to anyone who wants it.

This card symbolizes warmth, popularity, determination, positivity, optimism, self-assuredness, confidence, charisma, charm, enthusiasm and energy. The Queen of Wands relates to the astrological sign of Leo.

Reversed: A rigid, stubborn woman could try to block your progress. No matter what she does, keep calm, and do not discuss her or her motives with anyone else. Any gossiping you do will work to your disadvantage.

KING of WANDS

Description: A crowned king is sitting on his throne while holding a large flowering staff. A salamander is in the foreground by his left foot, and illustrations of three more salamanders and a lion can be seen on the panel behind the king's head. These salamanders are biting their own tails, which is a symbol of infinity. People used to believe that salamanders, who are amphibians that look like lizards, could not be hurt by fire, and consequently they are often used to represent the element of Fire. The lion symbolizes strength.

The King of Wands is a powerful and charismatic leader who encourages people to work with him to achieve worthwhile goals. He enjoys challenges, and is prepared to work as hard as anyone else to ensure success. The presence of this card is a sign that whatever you are currently working on can become successful. You need to decide what you want to achieve, set long-term goals, and then work hard until you've accomplished them. Right now you have the ability to take the leadership role, and inspire and motivate others.

This card symbolizes maturity, leadership, motivation, trust, inspiration, courage, originality, authority, decisiveness, respect, willpower, drive and passion. The King of Swords relates to the astrological sign of Aries.

Reversed: There's the likelihood of a disagreement with a person in authority. He is stubborn, unyielding, and fixed in his ways. Seek advice from people you trust to try to resolve this situation. A compromise is the most likely solution. However, you should refuse to give in if the matter involves anything you consider to be wrong.

THE SWORDS FAMILY

The suit of Swords relates to the element of Air, and this relates to thought, communication, logic, versatility and mental energy.

KNAVE of SWORDS

Description: A young man strides through a village holding his upraised sword in both hands. He appears calm and ready for anything.

The Knave of Swords is intelligent, quick-thinking, talkative and keen to learn as much as he can. He is full of enthusiasm and energy, and feels he can do anything he sets his mind on. He enjoys new ideas and theories, but lacks the experience and knowledge that comes from maturity. This card indicates a young person, or someone who is young at heart, who loves expressing him or herself while exploring new ideas, theories and philosophies. He or she needs to avoid idle gossip and speak the truth, as this is also a card of integrity.

This card symbolizes curiosity, communication, new ideas, honesty, justice, analysis, learning, fairness and responsibility.

Reversed: Someone will ask you to make a decision, while you're still unaware of all the facts. Refuse to act until you've investigated everything carefully. If you make a decision under pressure, you'll regret it later. Take time out for rest and relaxation to help release the pressure you're under.

KNIGHT of SWORDS

Description: A knight in armour and his white horse are galloping across a desolate landscape. The knight holds his sword high in his right hand as if charging into battle.

The Knight of Swords is full of drive, energy, ambition and determination. He has started on a project of some sort, and there is no stopping him as he is clearly focussed on his goal. He enjoys being busy and active. However, he may need to learn compassion, as he's unlikely to be aware of the motivations and needs of others. He has a good brain and excellent communication skills that he uses to his advantage. He never intends to harm others with his words, but as he tends to be blunt and say exactly what he means, he sometimes hurts others with what he says. He sees the world in black and white, and can't understand that other people see it from a different point of view.

This card symbolizes intelligence, focus, logic, authority, honesty, ambition, accomplishment, travel and activity. The Knight of Swords relates to the astrological sign of Gemini.

Reversed: This is not a good time to try to impress others by boasting or extravagant spending. You'll make a much better impression if you act modestly, and live within your means. This card also indicates that this is not a good time to start on anything new. Make plans, but delay the start until the current difficulties are behind you.

QUEEN of SWORDS

Description: A queen wearing a crown is sitting on her throne with an upraised sword in her right hand. Her left hand is raised in a gesture of acknowledgment, but she is looking downward and appears thoughtful, even unhappy. Behind her is what appears to be a harbour or lake.

The Queen of Swords is astute, logical and quick to grasp the essentials of a situation. She uses thought more than emotion when making decisions. She cares for others, but puts compassion to one side and uses her quick mind to speak the truth as she sees it. She willingly discusses anything with others, and enjoys guiding and helping them. However, she loses patience with people who are not prepared to help themselves. The Queen of Swords is believed to have suffered in love, but rather than becoming bitter about the experience, she used it to gain wisdom. Consequently, she offers good advice, using both logic and experience. She has also retained her sense of humour, which she uses to good effect to defuse difficult situations. Once you have all the necessary information, start using it to achieve your goals.

This card symbolizes experience, honesty, humour, intelligence, directness, good organisation, independence and subtlety. The Queen of Swords relates to the astrological sign of Aquarius.

Reversed: A narrow-minded, but influential, woman will not approve of your actions. Avoid dealing with her, if you can. If this is not possible, keep your dealings with her at a strictly professional level, and make sure to deliver what you promise. Be aware that she could be secretly trying to undermine you.

KING of SWORDS

Description: A fierce looking king wearing chainmail sits on his throne. He has a penetrating gaze that symbolizes his ability to grasp the essentials of a situation. He holds an upraised sword in his left hand.

The King of Swords is a strong authority figure. He is firm, honest, ethical and fair. He has the ability to see both sides of a situation, and once he has made up his mind, dispenses stern, impartial justice using logic and intellect. He may appear detached and remote, but his decisions and answers are based on great knowledge and experience. This card can indicate the need to obtain professional advice on something you're doing, or are planning to do. It also shows that you need to be calm, rational and rely on cold, hard facts at this time. The advice you receive will be fair and honest.

This card symbolizes authority, clarity of thought, insight, wisdom, honesty, analysis, justice, fair play and high standards. The King of Swords relates to the astrological sign of Libra.

Reversed: There's the possibility that you'll be treated unfairly and unjustly. Avoid confrontations, if possible, and obtain professional advice, if it proves necessary. Be careful who you confide in, and keep your emotions in check.

ASTROLOGY AND THE COURT CARDS

There are many different ways to associate Court Cards with Astrological Signs.

The method that follows is originated from a combination of the Suit elemental association, with the 3 modalities of Astrological Signs (Cardinal, Fixed and Mutable).

It is an useful and practical Method, but it's not the only one that can be used.

- Chalices: Water signs (Cancer, Scorpio, Pisces)
- Pentacles: Earth signs (Taurus, Virgo, Capricorn)
- Wands: Fire signs (Aries, Leo, Sagittarius)
- Swords: Air signs (Gemini, Libra, Acquarius)

- Cardinal signs: Queens (Aries, Cancer, Libra, Capricorn)
- Fixed signs: Kings (Taurus, Leo, Scorpio, Acquarius)
- Mutable signs: Knaves (Gemini, Virgo, Sagittarius, Pisces)

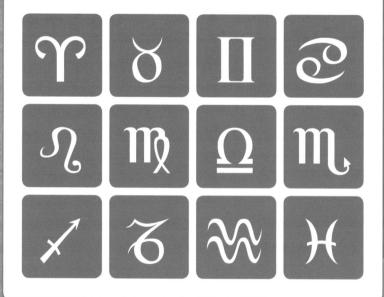

For those who are not Astrology expert, it could be useful to know that Cardinal signs (Queens) describe nurturing energies, excellent to start something and to grow, Fixed signs (Kings) describe solid, powerful energies, excellent for safety and achievement, Mutable signs (Knaves) describe flexible energies, excellent for adaptability and change.

- Queen of Wands – Aries (Cardinal Fire)
- King of Pentacles – Taurus (Fixed Earth)
- Knave of Swords – Gemini (Mutable Air)
- Queen of Chalices – Cancer (Cardinal Water)
- King of Wands – Leo (Fixed Fire)
- Knave of Pentacles – Virgo (Mutable Earth)
- Queen of Swords – Libra (Cardinal Air)
- King of Chalices – Scorpio (Fixed Water)
- Knave of Wands – Sagittarius (Mutable Fire)
- Queen of Pentacles – Capricorn (Cardinal Earth)
- King of Swords – Aquarius (Fixed Air)
- Knave of Chalices – Pisces (Mutable Chalices)

Within this Method, the Knights can be seen as the transitions between Seasons.

- Knight of Chalices – Spring to Summer – Summer Solstice
- Knight of Swords – Summer to Fall – Fall Equinox
- Knight of Pentacles – Fall to Winter – Winter Solstice
- Knight of Wands – Winter to Spring – Spring Equinox

TECHNIQUES

—w—

COMBINATIONS OF CARDS

The cards are dealt out in what is called a spread, or layout. Sometimes you'll notice that a particular number, or a certain court card figure, will appear a number of times in a spread. For instance, you may notice that there are three sevens or two knights in a spread. This has an effect on the reading. If two of these cards appear in the spread, it's a sign that two people will be involved in the outcome. Three cards indicate three or more people will be involved. Four cards is a good sign as it shows that the person is prepared to work hard and do the necessary groundwork to ensure success.

- *Two Aces:* This is a sign that a partnership or special relationship is likely to occur.
  Three Aces: This is a sign of good news. It can also mean that a group of people will be involved in the outcome.
  Four Aces: This indicates caution. The person will need to think matters through before making any important decisions.

- *Two Twos:* This indicates friendship or relationship.
  Three Twos: This is a sign of delays because of changes in plans.
  Four Twos: This is a positive indication that a number of people will be grouping together and working on a common goal.

- *Two Threes:* This is a neutral sign indicating news, novelties or new informations.
  Three Threes: This is a warning to avoid listening to, or spreading, gossip. Evaluate everything carefully, and make up your own mind before acting.
  Four Threes: This is a positive sign for people working on a group project. It indicates a successful conclusion.

- *Two Fours:* This is a positive sign of stability and safety.
  Three Fours: This is a sign that a great deal of time and effort will be required to achieve success.
  Four Fours: This is a sign of solid material success as a result of hard work.

- *Two Fives:* This is a sign of instability, conflict and competition.
  Three Fives: This is a sign to keep clearly focused on the ultimate goal, as the person will be diverted by other possibilities.
  Four Fives: This is a sign that other people could be trying to sabotage the person's efforts.

- *Two Six:* This is a sign of peace, indicating the presence of a serene environment where to develop creative ideas.
  Three Sixes: This is a sign that an important part of the project has been completed, and the people involved should celebrate this achievement.
  Four Sixes: This is a sign of peace, harmony and happiness. All relationships will improve.

- *Two Sevens:* This is a sign of an important experience to be made.
  Three Sevens: This is a sign of a successful conclusion to a situation that initially appeared impossible to resolve.
  Four Sevens: This is a sign of disappointments. The person being read for needs to think carefully before proceeding.

- *Two Eights:* This is a sign that indicates a journey, movement and inspiration.
  Three Eights: This is a positive sign. It's a sign that the person will be helped by someone else, and the result will be much better than if he or she had persevered without help. This can indicate a partnership or relationship.
  Four Eights: This is a sign of a great deal of hard work that has a financial payoff. All the time and effort put in will be rewarded.

- *Two Nines:* This is a sign – usually negative – of a discordance between wishes and reality.
  Three Nines: This is a sign of success, and usually indicates good health, prosperity and happiness.
  Four Nines: This is a sign of accomplishment and success. It hasn't happened easily, but the person can feel happy and elated at his or her accomplishment.

- *Two Tens:* This is a sign – usually positive – of different things coming together or perfect timing.
  Three Tens: This relates to the signing of important documents. It can relate to legal concerns.
  Four Tens: This is a powerful indicator of major success achieved through hard work, discipline and self-sacrifice.

- *Two Knaves:* This is a sign of a new friendship or relationship between two young people. There is likely to be much talk about the friendship.
  Three Knaves: This is a sign of enjoyable social activities involving young people.
  Four Knaves: This is a sign of friends meeting up with each other at social gatherings, and anywhere else where young people meet.

- *Two Knights:* This indicates a meeting of good friends.
  Three Knights: This is a sign of pleasant social activities involving people who are older than those depicted by Three Knaves.
  Four Knights: This is a sign of strong masculine energy in the situation the person is having a reading about. It's likely that they will influence the final result.

- *Two Queens:* This is a sign of jealousy, discord, suspicion and rivalry. The person needs to be careful who he or she trusts.
  Three Queens: This is a sign of women enjoying pleasant social times together. They are prepared to help anyone who requests it.
  Four Queens: This is a sign of women attending a formal function together. The occasion is serious, but the women are willing to offer the benefit of their knowledge and wisdom.

- *Two Kings:* This is a sign of a business partnership or relationship.
  Three Kings: This is a sign of men enjoying a pleasant social time together.
  Four Kings: This is a sign of important meetings with influential people.

HOW TO REMEMBER THE CARDS

It can seem daunting to look at a deck of Tarot cards for the first time and wonder how you'll possibly be able to remember them all. Fortunately, there are a number of ways to make the learning process easier.

PLAYING WITH THE CARDS

By far the simplest way is to play with the cards. Look through the deck and closely examine any cards that appeal to you. Look at the picture on the card and see if you can intuit enough information from it to help you discover the meaning of the card. Write your findings in a journal, so you can see how your interpretation differs from those you might have read. If you spent ten minutes a day doing this exercise, you'll learn the interpretations for all the cards in less than a month.

You might wonder if your interpretations are as good as those you might read in a book. Actually, they'll be better, as you've created them using intuition, imagination and logic. I know this is the case. A few years ago, a new Tarot deck arrived in the post just as I was leaving to catch up with a friend for a coffee. I took the cards with me, and studied them while waiting for my friend to arrive. I visit this cafe almost every day, and often read my Tarot cards there. Consequently, someone asked me for a reading, which I was happy to do. Other people were requesting readings when my friend arrived. I handed the cards to one of them and told them to ask a question and pull a card out of the deck. "It will answer your question," I told her. "Just look at the picture and see what it tells you." To my surprise, everyone who wanted a reading was able to have their question answered by the cards without my help. Ever since then, I've frequently let people read their own cards. If these people, who know nothing at all about the Tarot, can do this, so can you.

LEARNING THE MAJOR ARCANA

Throughout history, people have loved stories. Stories are one of the best ways to communicate information to others, as people tend to remember stories more than lists of facts or ideas. When I first started teaching the Tarot I found stories particularly helpful in helping people learn the basic meanings of each Tarot card.

Here's the story I used for the Major Arcana. You'll find it more useful if you read this with the Major Arcana cards in front of you, ideally arranged from *0 – The Fool* to *XXI – The World*. I like to hold the cards I'm referring to at each stage of the story.

0 – The Fool. "This is the story of a soul as it makes its way through life. This could be your soul, or my soul. In fact, it's everyone's soul. The soul is just beginning this incarnation. It's innocent. Look how happy the Fool looks as he sets off on his journey. He's got a bag full of knowledge, and he's carrying a rose to signify his love for everyone."

I – The Magician. "Now we move on to the Magician. He has the four elements of Fire, Earth, Air and Water visible on his table, symbolizing mind, body and spirit. He's standing in an 'as above, so below' position. His wand is pointing to the sky. Over his head is the infinity sign, which symbolizes eternal life. He's surrounded by roses and lilies. Lilies symbolize peace and purity. Roses symbolize love, in all its forms. Our soul is obviously armed with everything necessary for its epic journey. Of course, it has to decide what it does with these treasures."

II – The High Priestess. "The High Priestess is sitting serenely on her throne between the two pillars of wisdom. One is black, and the other white. This indicates good and evil. She's holding a scroll to symbolize knowledge. On the curtain behind her are pomegranates, which are symbols of fertility. The crescent moon at her feet symbolizes intuition and female wisdom."

III – The Empress. "The Empress sits in a beautiful garden with trees, lawns and even a stream. All of these symbolize fruitfulness and abundance. She looks pregnant – another symbol of fruitfulness. She's holding a sceptre to symbolize creativity. Beside her is a heart, probably the most popular symbol of love. Inside the heart is the symbol of Venus, another symbol of love."

IV – The Emperor. "The Emperor sits on a throne with his wand in one hand. He looks strong and powerful, which is as it should be, as he represents the masculine side of our natures, just as the Empress symbolizes the feminine. In fact, if you look at the Magician, the High Priestess, the Empress and the Emperor (look at them all) you can see our soul has everything required: the mental (the Magician), the spiritual (the High Priestess), female and male (the Empress and the Emperor).

V – The Hierophant. "The next card is the Hierophant. He represents conventional spiritual wisdom. He is blessing two people who are kneeling in front of him. The two keys in the foreground symbolize the keys to heaven."

VI – The Lovers. "The Lovers symbolize romantic love. They are being watched over, and protected, by an angel."

VII – The Chariot. "The Chariot symbolizes movement. The driver has no reins. Driving the chariot are two sphinxes, one white and one black. These symbolize the opposing energies and temptations the soul has to experience."

VIII – Strength. "This card is interesting, as it depicts a special sort of strength. Both the lady and the lion seem calm, serene and peaceful. The lady is gently closing the lion's jaws. This card symbolizes spiritual, or inner, strength. (Look at the Hierophant, the Lovers, the Chariot and Strength again.) The soul is progressing. It has learned to accept authority (the Hierophant). It is discovering the enduring power of love (the Lovers). It's discovering the temptations of different paths (the Chariot). And it has discovered it possesses all the inner strength (Strength) necessary to carry on."

IX – The Hermit. "The Hermit card shows the soul is pursuing a spiritual path. The lamp shines light on hidden wisdom. The soul is enjoying time on its own to contemplate, think, and gain an ever closer contact with the Divine."

X – The Wheel Of Fortune. "Change is the only constant in life, and this card represents that. On the left side of the wheel we have a serpent, symbolizing worldly concerns. On the right is Anubis, a jackal god of the ancient Egyptians. He symbolizes spiritual matters."

XI – Justice. "Justice shows that no matter how the Wheel of Fortune turns, everything works out eventually, and we all receive our due punishment or reward."

XII – The Hanged Man. "The Hanged Man is interesting. He's hanging upside down by one leg, yet seems perfectly happy. The halo around his head indicates spiritual growth. This card indicates the soul is gaining supremacy over the physical body. (Look at the Hermit, the Wheel of Fortune, Justice and the Hanged Man cards again.) These four cards indicate the soul's progress, despite the vagaries of the Wheel of Fortune."

XIII – Death. "This is the card that scares most people. There is no need for this, as it indicates that death is necessary for rebirth to occur. We need to discard the old and outmoded to progress on our spiritual path."

XIV – Temperance. "Temperance shows an angel pouring the water of life from one cup to another. This shows that even though the container may change, life carries on. Death is not the end."

XV – The Devil. "The Devil symbolizes the strong attraction worldly matters play in everyone's life. Yet, although the couple are chained to the pillar, which means they are chained to their earthly desires, it's a simple matter to break those bonds, and become free."

XVI – The Tower. "The Tower shows two people escaping from a tower that has been struck by lightning. This card symbolizes the 'lightning flash' of inspiration that can cause a sudden change, for good or ill. (Look at Death, Temperance, the Devil and the Tower cards again.) These cards show that the soul needs to be careful and not tie itself too much to worldly matters."

XVII – The Star. "The Star brings the promise that death is not the end. Everything in this card is blossoming, the vegetation, birds, the sky and even the giant star of hope. The beautiful girl is pouring the water of life onto the ground and into the pool of water."

XVIII – The Moon. "The Moon is a mystical card. Two dogs, or maybe a dog and a wolf, are baying at the moon. A crustacean is coming out of the water. In dreams, nothing is at it seems."

XIX – The Sun. "This is a card of joy, success, triumph and happiness. The young child is riding a white horse, which is a symbol of masculine energy. The banner rising to heaven symbolizes freedom from earthly concerns. All is well under the sun."

XX – Judgement. "Judgement shows an angel blowing a trumpet to invite us to rise up and start a new life, to realize that yesterday has gone, and a whole new world is waiting for us."

XXI – The World. "The World card shows a young lady holding two wands to represent her capabilities. She is surrounded by a laurel wreath, the symbol of triumph and success. In the four corners of this card are the four living creatures that surrounded God's throne in the Revelation of St. John the Divine. (Look at the Star, the Moon, the Sun, Judgement and the World cards again.) These cards show the star of hope guiding the soul through the darkness of night into the full light of day, so it can rise again and achieve its goal. And now, of course, (Look at the Fool card again.) the cycle begins again."

If you read this story several times with the cards in your hands, you'll learn the meanings of each Major Arcana card with no effort at all. I've mentioned before, and will probably say again, playing with the cards is the best way to learn them. Let the symbols in the cards speak to you. If you're anything like me, you'll find yourself falling in love with the cards. Once you reach this stage, you'll be amazed at the insights that come to you when you're giving readings for others.

THE MINOR ARCANA

After discovering how useful a story could be in teaching people the Major Arcana, it made sense to create stories to help people remember the meanings of the Minor Arcana cards, too. You'll find it easier in the long run if you become familiar with the Major Arcana cards before starting to memorise the Minor Arcana. The major difference between these stories and the Major Arcana story is that these do not include the interpretations of each card. I'm using descriptions of the cards to help you visualize each card. Once you've read through each story several times, you should be able to visualize each card in your mind whenever you wish, even if you don't have your Tarot cards with you. The next section will help you remember the meanings of each Minor Arcana card.

As you did with the story of the Major Arcana, you should read the stories of the four suits with the cards in front of you.

Chalices

Mr and Mrs Chalice (King and Queen of Chalices) have two sons, Knight (Knight of Chalices) and Knave (Knave of Chalices). Knight wants to settle down and have a family (Ten of Chalices), but Knave lives for the day and generally drinks to excess every night (Nine of Chalices). Knight moves away from home to seek his fortune (Eight of Chalices). Knave weaves elaborate fantasies and dreams, and then has another drink (Seven of Chalices). Knight finds his childhood sweetheart (Six of Chalices). At about the same time, Knave wakes up with a terrible hangover and re-evaluates his life (Five of Chalices). Knight finds his childhood sweetheart has changed, and is no longer the person he remembered (Four of Chalices). He finds Knave and together they go to a party (Three of Chalices) where they both meet wonderful women (Two of Chalices). A hand comes out of the clouds holding a cup to show that love rules over all (Ace of Chalices).

Pentacles

A wealthy man (King of Pentacles) and his wife (Queen of Pentacles) have two sons (Knight and Knave of Pentacles). The younger son pursues an attractive woman, promising her riches beyond compare (Ten of Pentacles). The woman is tempted, and starts living the high life (Nine of Pentacles). The older son works hard in his father's business (Eight of Pentacles). He is patient (Seven of Pentacles) and generous (Six of Pentacles). In the meantime, his brother has wasted his fortune (Five of Pentacles). The woman leaves him and he is left alone, clutching his last few coins (Four of Pentacles). The older brother finds him, and suggests he starts pursuing a natural talent he's always had (Three of Pentacles). The younger brother starts earning money, and has to decide how much to save, and how much to spend (Two of Pentacles). The younger brother has learned his lesson, and the two brothers combine forces to build up the family business still further (Ace of Pentacles).

Wands

The King and Queen of Wands have a son they are very proud of (Knight of Wands). He is deeply in love with a princess in a nearby country, but unfortunately there is also another suitor (Knave of Wands). He tries to impress the princess with his strength (Ten of Wands). This does not work. While he is thinking what to do next (Nine of Wands) he is attacked (Eight of Wands). He defeats his rival (Seven of Wands) and decides to propose to his sweetheart (Six of Wands). The other suitor is not ready to give up, and forces him into an unfair fight (Five of Wands). The princess sees how honest and ethical he is compared to the dastardly tactics of the other suitor. She marries him, and he takes her home to his castle (Four of Wands). With the love of a good woman to support him, he looks for new worlds to conquer (Three of Wands). In time, his kingdom takes up much of the globe (Two of Wands), and his beneficial reign enriches everyone (Ace of Wands).

Swords

The King, Queen and Knight of swords rule a kingdom that has been experiencing a civil war. The Knave of Swords is a young man who enters the king's service. Unfortunately, the king's son is murdered (Ten of Swords). His sister wakes up from a nightmare (Nine of Swords) that tells her what's happened to her brother. She resolves to capture his murderer. She is kidnapped, bound and kept prisoner (Eight of Swords). The lowly Knave sets off to rescue her (Seven of Swords). He is secretly in love with her. He has to travel far and wide (Six of Swords), but eventually finds and fights the enemy (Five of Swords). He thinks he's defeated them, but they come back and kill him (Four of Swords). The sister escapes and she and her parents are broken-hearted as they realize, too late, the Knave's devotion (Three of Swords). The sister swears vengeance, and is blind to any thoughts of peace (Two of Swords). The Ace of Swords, appearing from a cloud, shows that people who live by the sword, die by the sword.

You don't need to limit yourself to my stories. You might like to create your own stories for each of the suits. You might even select ten or twelve cards randomly, and create a story using them. It's fun to do, and it will help you learn the cards quickly and effortlessly. Interestingly, many writers use spreads of Tarot cards to help them plot their books. Although this is done largely by writers of fantasy novels, I've met fiction writers of all sorts who find the cards helpful to them in plotting their books.

THE NUMBERS AND THE SUITS

If you combine the meanings of each number with the different suits, you'll find you'll quickly come up with your own interpretations for each card.

1 – The Aces. The Aces all signify new beginnings, and show that it's time for the person consulting the cards to take action and move forward. The Aces indicate the start of a new cycle, and show that something is about to start. It's a time to plant seeds.

2 – The Twos. The Twos relate to harmony, balance, relationships, and getting along well with others. It frequently indicates a partnership. It can also relate to waiting for matters to develop.

3 – The Threes. Three is the number of joy, communication, growth, and creative self-expression. The Three of Wands, Chalices and Pentacles are all happy cards, expressing the fun-loving, positive aspects of this number. The Three of Swords is the odd one out. It still signifies communication, but this is in the form of disagreements and arguments.

4 – The Fours. The Fours relate to making a good, solid foundation to build on. It is the start of the manifestation that has come about through hard work, good organization, and planning. The Fours also indicate a time to pause and reflect before moving forward again.

5 – The Fives. The Fives indicate changes (that can be good or bad), instability, and the inevitable ups and downs of life. They usually have a negative connotation.

6 – The Sixes. The Sixes relate to harmony, balance, compassion, love, service, responsibility and adjustment.

7 – The Sevens. The Sevens are inward looking and relate to introspection, dreams, soul-searching, wisdom, mysticism and faith.

8 – The Eights. The Eights indicate power, perseverance, practicality and positive potential. The Eight of Swords might seem to go against this, but once she removes her blindfold and frees herself, this woman can move ahead.

9 –The Nines. The Nines indicates the person being read for is nearing the end of a cycle of experience. They also relate to tolerance, selflessness, idealism, and helping others.

10 – The Tens. The Tens mark the transition from one experience to another. It marks the end of one cycle of experience, and the planning and initial stages of the next. This is usually an important change.

The Chalices. The suit of Chalices relates to feelings and emotions. Consequently, joy, happiness, friendship, love, creativity and spirituality are all connected with this suit. The element associated with the suit of Chalices is Water.

The Pentacles. The suit of Pentacles relates to material gain and financial security. The element associated with the suit of Pentacles is Earth.

The Wands. The suit of Wands relates to enthusiasm, energy, ambition, hard work and travel. The element associated with the suit of Wands is Fire.

The Swords. The suit of Swords relates to power, obstacles, courage and the power of the mind. The element associated with the suit of Swords is Air.

Here are two examples of the interpretations that can be made by combining the number and the suit. If you combine, for example, the number Two with the suit of Chalices, you create the Two of Chalices. This obviously relates to relationships, and could indicate a love affair, friendship, or even a business partnership.

Number Ten and the suit of Swords creates the Ten of Swords. The indicates the ending of a difficult situation. The person having the reading has been through a difficult time, but the situation is about to improve, especially if he or she learns from the experience and becomes stronger as a result.

—✺—

PREDICTING THE FUTURE

Most people buy a deck of tarot cards as they want to gain a glimpse into the future. This is called divination. Because the future is uncertain, we all have times when it would be wonderful to know what was going to happen next week or next month. However, this isn't possible as the future isn't fixed, and we all possess free will. Interestingly enough, the opposite argument can also be made: if our fate is fixed we would be unable to predict it. At first glance, this seems impossible, yet I can demonstrate it with a story.

Imagine that someone is about to take a plane trip to another country. On the day before the trip, he visits a fortune-teller who tells him that the plane will crash and he'll be killed. Once he leaves, the man thinks about his two choices. He can either cancel the flight and stay at home, or he could take the flight and be killed. If the future really is fixed, he'll take the flight and be killed. However, that would never happen because, no one would deliberately board a flight knowing he was going to be killed. If the man had even the slightest degree of free will, he'd cancel the flight, continue living, and change his entire future.

Predicting the future was explained to me very simply many years ago by a man who told me the future is fan-shaped. When I asked him to explain that, he told me a story. A bushman in Africa has spent the day hunting. The day is coming to an end and he has to return home. There are two possible routes. If he takes one of the paths he'll get home safely, and be able to enjoy the evening with his wife and family. If he takes the other path he won't get home at all, as he'll be eaten by a lion. The side edges of the fan illustrate these two possible paths, and the person who is reading the cards has to provide advice about which of the paths to choose.

Fortunately, most of our decisions don't involve life or death. All the same, it can be useful to have an oracle of some sort that can shine a light on different aspects of our problem. Although this oracle won't be able to predict the future with 100% precision, it can provide insights into how we feel and think about the situation, and this added information can make it easier to make the right decision. The oracle helps your conscious mind gain access to information that you already know at a deeper, subconscious level.

—ᴍ—

YOUR FIRST READINGS

Your first readings are likely to be stilted and awkward. This is natural. Anything worthwhile takes time and practice. I remember the long silences I had in my early readings as I struggled to think of the right words to explain what I saw in the cards. However, fluency gradually came, and my readings became smoother and more effective. In the early stages, it's important to tell people that you're still learning the cards. Although they'll thank you for their readings, in many ways you should be thanking them for giving you the opportunity to practice.

Once you start reading with your cards, you'll discover that it's harder to read for yourself than it is to read for someone else. This is because we all have our own specific hopes, dreams and fears about the future, and these hinder our desire to be objective when we read our own cards. It's hard to be impartial when you're emotionally involved in the outcome. In fact, if you do have an emotional involvement in the situation, it's better to ask someone else to read the cards for you, rather than try to do a reading yourself.

If you intend using your cards to read for other people you must possess a genuine desire to help others. You need to be sympathetic, understanding, empathetic and kind. You also need to be discreet. The people you read for are likely to open up and tell you all sorts of things they wouldn't normally divulge to anyone. You need to be like a doctor or priest and keep anything you learn during your readings secret.

READING FOR YOURSELF

I know more people who read for themselves, than people who read for others. Consequently, the chances are high that most of your readings will be for yourself. This is wonderful, as your Tarot deck will become a valuable guide that will help you in everything you do. Many people consult the Tarot when matters are not going well in their lives. However, you should consult the Tarot even when everything is going your way, as it will provide valuable insights that can warn you of problems ahead, or even how to make an existing good situation even better.

Ideally, you should create a ritual around your Tarot cards. If you have time, you can create a ritual incorporating favourite objects as well as your cards. However, this may not be possible if you're choosing a Card of the Day in the morning in a small period of time before leaving for work. Even then, you can create a small ritual by sitting on the same chair every morning, taking a few slow deep breaths, and holding the cards in your hands for a few moments before shuffling them, choosing one, and then reading it. A one-card reading is perfect in this type of situation, as you can carry the card with you throughout the day, and interpret it whenever you have time.

In the weekends, when you have more time, you might create a sacred space and read for yourself there. This can be anywhere where you won't be disturbed for the length of time you require. I enjoy reading my cards outdoors, Doing this gets me away from the phone and other potential interruptions, and I can think about what I'm going to ask the Tarot while walking to my sacred space.

Although I regularly read the cards for myself, I occasionally ask someone else to read the cards for me. I do this whenever I need good, sound advice and don't want my feelings about the situation to get in the way.

PREPARING TO READ

Many readers like to spend a few moments on their own before reading the cards. This enables them to get comfortable, quieten their minds, and relax. It's a form of meditation that enables them to get in touch with their inner wisdom and open up a spiritual connection with the universe. Some readers like to hold the deck of Tarot cards while imagining a pure white light descending from above that eliminates negativity and and surrounds them with protection. I enjoy setting out my reading cloth and other items before doing a reading. It's a small ritual that gets my mind clearly focussed on the reading I'm about to do.

It doesn't matter what you choose to do as long as it gets you in the right state of mind to do the reading. The purpose of a short ritual before reading the cards is to enable you to become centred and separated from your everyday concerns.

WHERE TO READ THE CARDS

You can read the cards for yourself anywhere you happen to be. However, if you're doing a reading for someone else, it's best to do it somewhere quiet and private, with only the two of you present. You might be fortunate enough to have a room that you use largely for your readings. In this case, you can display pictures and surround yourself with anything that holds special meaning for you. Even if you don't have a designated area for your readings, you can create a comfortable space by displaying a crystal, a reading cloth, or anything else that helps you get into the right state of mind before sitting down to read.

THE QUESTION

The first thing you need to do before doing a tarot spread is to formulate a question. This needs to be a sincere, serious question. If you don't want to know the answer to a question, don't ask it. This seems obvious, but many people ask questions and are disappointed with what the Tarot tells them. Ideally, the question needs to be one that you want answered because the information will be useful to you in making plans and decisions.

Questions need to be framed carefully. You should avoid questions that require a 'yes' or 'no' answer. Don't ask questions that include the word "ever," such as, "Will I ever be happy?"

You can put a time limit on your questions. If you're intending to start a new business, for instance, you might ask, "Will I start my business between now and January 1st?"

Whenever possible, you should ask open-ended questions. Instead of, for instance, asking "When will I get married?", you should ask something along the lines of "What would be the best way for me to meet the person of my dreams?", or "What is preventing me from meeting the right person for me?"

SHUFFLING THE CARDS

The cards are usually mixed while the question is being formulated. You can mix the cards in any way you wish. If you've ever played games with regular playing cards, you might mix the cards by holding them in your hands and shuffling them. However, as Tarot cards are large than regular playing cards, you might find it easier to shuffle the cards from the ends, rather than the sides.

You might prefer to spread the cards face down on a table and mix them together before picking them up. Alternatively, you can spread the cards and then pick them up one at a time, choosing them randomly from different positions on the table.

Another method is to cut the cards into two piles and rotate both of them to create two rosettes. If you then push the two piles into each other, they'll automatically mix themselves as you form one pile of cards.

If the question has already been determined, you should think of the question while shuffling the cards.

THE ANSWER

The tarot cards do not provide specific answers. They provide perspective and a fresh way of looking at the situation, but usually do not say anything specific. Consequently, you should never tell your client that the cards say such-and-such will happen, as the outcome may well be completely different. Your clients have free will and the information provided by the cards will help them make their own decisions.

CLARIFICATION CARDS

There'll be occasions when you'll find that a card fails to give you a clear answer. When this occurs you can draw another card from the deck and place it overlapping the card you wish to clarify. Read this card, in association with the card that caused confusion, and see if the combination provides greater clarity.

This situation usually arises when you're doing a spread involving a number of cards. If it occurs when you're doing a one-card spread, ask another question relating to the first card as you draw the second card from the deck.

Some readers like to mix the cards again before drawing a clarification card. Others – and I'm one of them – don't bother. You should do whatever feels best for you at the time.

SIGNIFICATOR CARDS

A significator card is a card that signifies either the person having the reading, or the question that is being asked. Some readers always choose a significator card to represent the client before every reading. Other readers don't bother. There are pros and cons to both methods. significator cards were almost always used in the first half of the Twentieth Century. This reflects the influence of Arthur Edward Waite, the creator of the Rider-Waite Tarot deck. However, many people nowadays feel that removing one card from the deck could affect the outcome of the reading, as that card is effectively not available to be interpreted. I use a significator card only when doing the Celtic Cross spread, which you'll read later. I do this solely because it's traditional, and was the way I was originally taught this spread. Nowadays, many people do this spread without using a significator card.

The easiest way to choose a significator card is to ask the person having the reading to select one of the court cards that he or she feels most closely resembles him or her. If none of the court cards appeal, the significator can be chosen using the person's astrological sign.

- If the person belongs to a **Fire sign** (Aries, Leo, Sagittarius) he or she could choose any card from the suit of **Wands**.
- If the person belongs to an **Earth sign** (Taurus, Virgo, Capricorn) he or she could choose any card from the suit of **Pentacles**.
- If the person belongs to an **Air sign** (Gemini, Libra, Aquarius) he or she could choose any card from the suit of **Swords**.
- If the person belongs to a **Water sign** (Cancer, Scorpio, Pisces) he or she could choose any card from the suit of **Chalices**.

To save time, I usually select the Significator card. I do this by choosing one of the court cards that relates to his or her horoscope sign.

DETERMINING TIME

It's extremely difficult to tell when a specific event will happen. However, the cards often provide a clue. If you're asking a question about the timing of a certain event, and draw a card from the Major Arcana, it's a sign that the event will occur in the near future.

The Knaves, Queens and Kings of the Court cards are all related to astrological signs that indicate the months in which the event could occur. The Knights have no astrological significance as they indicate sudden changes and action.

Cards from the Minor Arcana often provide the season of the year it which it will occur. Minor Arcana cards also denote days or weeks. If, for instance, you draw the Six of Pentacles, the event could occur within six days or weeks.

Some people use the Aces to signify seasons. The Ace of Pentacles indicates Spring, the Ace of Chalices indicates Summer, the Ace of Wands indicates Autumn, and the Ace of Swords indicates Winter.

Please remember, however, that the interpretation of a card when referring to timing cannot be set with rules, as it is very dependent on the question asked. If the question is something like "what is the best time of the year to make a journey?", extracting a single minor Arcana and interpreting it as the season can be a suitable technique. However, if the question is something like "what is the the best time of the week to invite my friends for dinner?" the same technique would not be appropriate.

When in doubt, a very simple way to address timing questions, is just to use the following rule of thumb.
- Numeral Cards: 1 means very soon, while 10 means very late.
- Court Cards: means that the timing depend on a person.
- Major Arcana: the event will verify soon after something connected to the chosen Arcana will happen. For instance, if the Arcana is the Lover, the correct timing will be after a choice has been taken (Lovers = Choice).

If this technique is too complicated, it's possible to draw cards until a numeral card appear and then read it, ignoring the previous Courts or Majors.

TAROT REVERSALS

When the cards are mixed it's possible for cards to turn upside down. These are called Tarot Reversals. Some readers like to have reversed cards in their spreads and deliberately shuffle their decks with some cards upright and others upside down. Other readers do the opposite and turn any reversed cards upright. Some readers don't interpret the upside down cards in a different way, but pay particular attention to them, as they have marked themselves out by being reversed. Because Tarot Reversals are controversial, they are a popular topic of conversation whenever Tarot card readers meet.

This is not a new debate. Etteilla (the pseudonym of a French occultist named Jean-Baptiste Alliette) wrote that many Parisian card readers were interpreting card reversals as far back as 1753.

I have provided the reversed meanings in case you wish to use them. However, it's up to you to decide whether or not to use the interpretations for reversed cards.

DROPPED CARDS

It's an important sign if a card drops or appears to jump out of the deck while you're shuffling it. This card has made itself visible for a reason, and should be studied carefully. Often this card will provide the answer to the question, and there'll be no need to continue with the rest of the reading. Even if it doesn't answer the question, this card will play a role in the reading. Consequently, it should never be ignored.

SPREADS

The spread is the layout of cards. This can be as simple as one card randomly selected from a shuffled deck of cards. You can also go to the opposite extreme and do a spread that uses all 78 cards in the deck. I haven't ever felt the need to use an entire deck of tarot cards in a single spread, as I feel it would confuse the issue, but have met people who use nothing else.

The spread also adds structure to the reading. If, for instance, you are doing a three card spread, with one card indicating the past, the second the present, and the third the future, the interpretation of the card placed in each position will change according to its position. Each position in the spread provides a component of the answer.

The energies of cards placed close to or next to each other in a spread interact, and this affects the interpretation, too. You'll need to use your intuition to help you decide if the blend of energies is positive, neutral or negative. You'll find that your intuition will expand the more you work with your cards.

We'll start with a one card spread and then move on to more complex layouts. You'll probably find that one particular spread appeals to you more than the others. If so, use it. Experiment with the other spreads, too, but work with the one that resonates best for you. I find that I use a particular spread for a length of time, and then, for no apparent reason discover that I've started using a completely different spread. This happens with no conscious thought on my part, and I believe I'm using the right spread for me, and my clients, at that particular time.

ONE CARD SPREAD

Obviously, this is the easiest spread of all, but it is no less useful because of that. All you need to do is to think about your question while mixing the cards. Once you've asked your question, spread the cards in your hands facedown, and remove one. You might prefer to place the cards face down on a table and cut them in half, placing the cards you cut off the deck under the others. Pick up the new top card and interpret it. Alternatively, after mixing the cards, deal yourself the top card of the deck.

A good way to get to know the meanings of all the cards is to ask the question, "What will I learn today?" when you get out of bed in the morning. Carry the card with you during the day, and look at it whenever you have a spare moment. In the evening, look at the card while thinking about the day you've had, and see how relevant it was to what actually occurred.

Here's an example. Let's suppose you drew the Three of Pentacles from your tarot deck this morning. You looked at the card and noticed the two important men watching the young man work on his sculpture. You may have had a chance to look at the card two or three times during the day, but didn't think much about it until you were getting ready for bed. You realised that during the day you and your colleagues had been working on an important project at work. At one stage you'd felt you were doing more than your fair share of the work, but that feeling had passed when a supervisor commented favourably on what you were doing. The Three of Pentacles had effectively predicted the sort of day you were going to have.

Many people think that one-card readings are only for minor problems. However, as there is so much symbolism and meaning in every card, they can be used for any concern you or your clients might experience. Many years ago, someone told me that having a one-card reading was like discussing a problem with a wise old friend. He or she would listen sympathetically, and then provide insights and ideas that you hadn't even considered. A one-card spread is like that. It enables you to see a difficulty from a different point of view, and this provides clarity and fresh information.

One-card readings can be used in different ways. I often use it to determine what I should do next when I'm faced with a particular concern. You might also ask it to give you information on the cause of the problem, the main person involved, what one specific action should you do, or the outcome. Earlier, I suggested using it to provide information about the present day. You could extend this to a week, a month, or even longer, if you wish.

THREE CARD SPREADS

The three-card spread is a popular one with tarot card readers as it is easy to cast, and is extremely versatile. The most common three card spread is Past, Present and Future. The first card dealt reveals something significant from the past that is affecting the current situation. The second card helps to clarify the present moment, and the third card provides information about the possible outcome if the situation remains as it is.

After the cards have been mixed, the top three cards are dealt face up in a row. If you wish, instead of using the top three cards you could cut the deck into three piles and turn over the top card of each pile.

The three card spread is versatile, and is not restricted to past, present and future readings. You could, for instance, use it to examine relationships by doing: You, The Other Person and The Relationship. If you have a question you might use: Yes, No and Maybe to put fresh light on the situation.

Here are some other possibilities:
* Morning, Afternoon and Evening
* Current Situation, Obstacle and Advice
* Goal, Obstacle and Solution
* Opportunities, Challenges and Outcome
* Mind, Body and Spirit
* You, Partner and Problem
* Problem, What should I do? and Outcome
* Date in the Past, Present Date and Date in the Future (These could be Yesterday, Today and Tomorrow, Last Month, This Month and Next Month, or might be specific dates such as February 14th, March 23rd, and April 2nd.)

Here's an example of a three card spread. Let's assume you're a woman in your late twenties, you're unattached, you've met a young man and feel that you're falling in love. Your major problem is that he lives two hundred kilometres away, and you'll have to move to his city if the relationship progresses and becomes permanent. You could do a three card spread with one card indicating you, the second card the other person, and the third card the relationship. You might ask a specific question, such as: "Is he the right man for me?" You could also do a Past, Present and Future reading to see what it had to say about the relationship.

As this is a relationship question, let's cast three cards to indicate you, the man in question, and the relationship. After shuffling the deck while thinking about your question concerning the relationship, you deal three cards: the Seven of Wands, the Eight of Pentacles and Temperance.

The first card indicates you. The Seven of Wands shows that you're being forced to stand up for yourself. Perhaps close friends and family are unhappy about the proposed relationship as it means you'll be moving away. There could be another woman who is interested in pursuing a relationship with your man. It's likely that you'll know what the particular problem or concern is. The good thing about the Seven of Wands in this position is that it shows you will succeed in your goal.

The second card is the Eight of Pentacles. It looks as if most of your partner's time and energy are going into his career. He's motivated, ambitious and eager to learn. He's progressing, and his work is being noticed by others.

The third card is Temperance. This card represents the relationship. As Temperance symbolizes moderation, it's an indication that the relationship will develop slowly, and you (and your partner) will need to communicate openly with each other and be patient until the time is right to move ahead more quickly.

It looks as if the relationship will continue to grow and develop. Your partner is more interested in his career than anything else at the moment, but as long as you and he are prepared to allow the relationship to develop at its own pace, the two of you will ultimately be very happy together.

FIVE CARD SPREAD

This spread provides more detail than the three card spread. It uses the Past, Present and Future, but includes two additional cards: Mystery and Suggestions. The cards are shuffled and dealt out in a row. The first card is the Past, the second indicates the Present, the third reveals any Mysteries, the fourth provides Suggestions, and the fifth is the Future.

The Mystery card indicates anything that is hidden, secret, or possibly overlooked. The Suggestions card provides possible ideas on the next step or two you need to take.

Let's assume you're reading for someone who is unhappy in his career and wants to move into a completely different field. He is forty years old, and married with three young children. His current job pays well, but he feels he's in a rut. His hobby is photography and he'd like to set up his own studio.

He shuffles the cards, and hands them back to you. You cut the cards and deal out five cards in a row in front of him. If he's sitting opposite you, you deal the cards from your right to your left. This means the first card dealt is on your client's left.

Let's assume the cards are the Three of Pentacles, the Nine of Swords, the King of Swords, the Nine of Wands and the Nine of Chalices.

You briefly explain what the five positions indicate, and then look at the card representing the past. "In the past," you might say, "You worked hard to develop your skills. You got on well with the people you worked with, and you probably received recognition for your abilities early on. You might have needed to learn some patience, as you were keen to climb the ladder of success."

"This card indicates the present situation," you say, touching the Nine of Swords. "As you can see, this is not a happy card. The woman in the card has woken up from a nightmare and can't get back to sleep. It's the middle of the night, and her thoughts are full of fear, anxiety and worry. This card tells me that you're wallowing in negative thoughts, and you need to somehow turn them around. You are the one creating these thoughts, and they're making your life miserable. They must also be affecting your whole family.

"This card – the King of Swords – indicates anything that's hidden, concealed, or maybe forgotten. The King of Swords is an interesting card in this position. You either have a strong man in your life, someone who can see both sides of a situation and will give you honest, impartial feedback, or you need to find the best professional advice you can. It's also a sign that you need to rely on facts, and don't let yourself get carried away by hopes and dreams. You need to be realistic. Is there such a person in your life?"

Readings are usually conversations between the reader and the client, and the client would probably have identified the man, or the need for professional advice, before I asked the question. Sometimes you need to ask questions to encourage the client to speak. We'll assume that the client has completely overlooked the need for proper advice.

"The fourth card is the Nine of Wands. This is the card that gives you an indication about what you should do next. It's an interesting card. It shows that you're struggling from external pressures. I imagine your family will be a factor here. The good thing is that this is a card of persistence, and success after a struggle. It shows that you have the necessary drive and persistence to follow your dream and make it happen. You should explain exactly what you're planning to do to everyone who's involved, especially your wife. Once you get them onside, you'll move forward much more easily.

"Before we discuss the final card, have you noticed that there are three nines in the spread? The Nine of Swords, the Nine of Wands and the Nine of Chalices. This is a fortunate grouping as far as your reading is concerned, as it relates to the realization of your goals. Three nines in a spread usually relate to health, happiness and financial success. It can also indicate three or more people involved in helping you achieve your goal.

"Now we come to the final card. This is the card that indicates the likely outcome. It's not set in stone, as you possess free will and may change your mind. Naturally, this would change the outcome. Even when the Future card is positive, as this one is, you'll still need to do be clearly focused and work hard to ensure the positive result eventuates. You have the Nine of Chalices in this position. As you can see, the man on the card is enjoying an extremely happy and successful lifestyle. The Nine of Chalices is the 'wish' card, as it shows that what the person has wished for will become real. It won't happen easily, but if you get good professional advice, set yourself some worthwhile goals, get your family behind you, and follow through, you'll make a success of your photography business."

ELEMENTAL SPREAD

This is another five card spread that I find useful, as it helps clarify a situation using the four elements. I find this spread helpful for people who have already decided on what they're going to do, and want to find out how this decision affects different areas of their lives.

The first card is dealt facing north. This direction relates to the element of Earth. The next three cards are dealt in a clockwise direction facing east (Air), south (Fire) and west (Water). The final card is placed in the centre.

The cards are then interpreted. The first card (Earth) provides information on how the situation affects the person asking the question physically, practically or financially. The second card (Air) provides information on how the situation is affecting the person's thoughts and communications. The third card (Fire) provides information on how the situation affects the person's creativity, desires and needs. The fourth card (Water) provides information on how the situation is affecting the person's feelings, emotions, relationships and spirituality. The final card indicates the expected outcome if the person continues on the path he or she is already on.

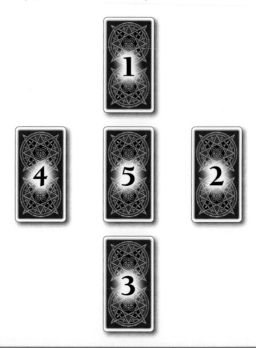

QUESTION ANSWERING SPREAD

This is a useful way to answer a series of questions that all relate to the same concern. I find it helpful to make a list of questions, as it's easy to forget to ask them all when you're relying solely on your memory. However, I don't feel limited by the list. If another question occurs to me while doing this spread, I always ask it.

You start by mixing the cards while thinking of your main concern. You continue mixing the cards while reading, and preferably speaking out loud, your first question that relates to the concern. When you've finished reading or saying the question you stop mixing the cards and deal the top card of the face down deck onto a table. Put the deck of cards down and turn over the card you've just dealt. It should provide insights into the question. If this card makes you think of another question, write it down on your list of questions. Mix the cards again while thinking (or speaking) your second question. When you've done this, deal the new top card onto the table beside the first card you dealt. Turn it over and interpret it while relating it to your question. Continue doing this until all the questions have been answered. If you had seven questions, you'll finish with seven face up cards lined up in a row on the table. If you had five questions, you'll have five cards on the table, and so on.

By now you'll have gained some insight into your main concern, as each card will have provided information about the questions surrounding the concern. Now you can read the cards again as a group. Think of your main concern, and then read the cards from left to right. Remember that these cards do not tell the story from the past to the future, as each one was drawn to answer a specific question. If you wish, you can deal one more card to represent the final outcome.

THE OPTIONS SPREAD

This is a useful spread to use if you have to make a choice between two possibilities, and are unsure which one to take. One card is dealt to indicate the present situation. Below this card are dealt two columns, each containing three cards. The left-hand column indicates one possibility, and the other column denotes the second possibility.

I recently did this spread for a friend who had a good position in a software development company. However, he'd always dreamed of making his living as an entertainer. A resort hotel had offered him a fulltime position entertaining their guests. The money they offered was less than half what he was earning at the computer company. However, it gave him the opportunity to get started in a field he loved, and if he did well, his income would increase. He was torn between the two options, and asked me for a reading to clarify the situation. The Options Spread was the perfect spread for his situation.

After mixing and cutting the cards, my friend dealt out seven cards. The Eight of Pentacles went into the Present Situation position, three cards went into the first possibility: the Four of Pentacles, the Ten of Wands and the Four of Chalices, and the remaining three cards created the second possibility column: the Ace of Swords, the Eight of Wands and the World.

"The Eight of Pentacles indicates the present situation," I told my friend. "It's an interesting card as it relates well to both possibilities. It shows that you are focused, willing to work hard, and experience great satisfaction whenever you achieve a worthwhile goal. You've been successful in your current job, and you're prepared to put your hard work ethic into a new career.

"This first column gives us some information about what would be likely to happen if you stayed in your current career. The Four of Pentacles is a sign that you shouldn't hang on too tightly to what you've already achieved. There could be a reluctance to let go because of the risks involved in trying something new.

"The Ten of Wands shows you're weighed down with responsibilities, and are working too hard. If you stay where you are, you're going to have to learn how to delegate, as you're doing too much yourself.

"The Four of Chalices shows that you're dissatisfied, and want a change. You might be bored, and feel hemmed in and restricted. It looks as if you find it hard to think of any good things about your current position, even though you know you're doing a good job, and everyone is happy with what you're doing.

"Let's look at the other possibility. This is what's likely to happen if you change careers and become an entertainer. The first card is the Ace of Swords. That's a sign of a new beginning, which is what would happen if you decide to take this path. It's an extremely powerful card, and it could almost indicate that change is inevitable.

"The next card is the Eight of Wands. This indicates an exciting stage in your life with plenty of opportunities to explore. If you take this path, this card indicates that your progress will be a joy to behold.

"The final card is the World. This is the card of worldly success, and shows that you'll not only reach your goals, but will be well rewarded as a result. After celebrating your success, you'll be offered future opportunities to expand your career even further."

My friend was a student of the Tarot, and had a huge smile on his face before I even started talking about the second possibility. "Thank you very much," he said. "You've told me exactly what I needed to hear." His family were not thrilled with his decision, and his mother told him he was a "dreamer." However, after looking at the cards in his spread, I'm confident he'll do well in his new career.

MAJOR ARCANA SPREAD

As its name indicates, this six-card spread uses only the cards of the Major Arcana. I use this spread when I need the answer to an important question.

The cards are mixed and cut into three piles. The top card of each pile is dealt to create a horizontal row of three cards. If I'm reading the cards for myself, I create a second row of cards below the first using the new top cards of each pile. If I'm reading the cards for someone else, he or she mixes the cards again, cuts them into three piles, and deals the top card of each pile to create a row below the row I created. By the end of this process, there are two rows, each containing three cards, on the table.

The three cards in the top row are read first, from left to right. The first card indicates the person having the reading. The second card reveals the essentials of the situation, and the third card indicates anything that could prove helpful. The three cards in the second row are read in the same order. The first indicates anything unforeseen that could occur, the second relates to the subconscious wishes of the person having the reading, and the final card indicates a possible outcome.

Let's assume you're reading the cards for a middle-aged woman who had not communicated with her mother for thirty years. She's not sure whether or not she should make contact, but as her mother is now elderly, she can't keep putting any decision off indefinitely. The six cards dealt are: the Hermit, the Fool, Strength, the Lovers, the Hierophant and Temperance.

"The first card represents you," you might say, indicating the Hermit card. "This shows that you've needed a great deal of time to reflect on your past relationship with your mother. You've probably learned a great deal as you've contemplated and thought about it. No matter what the rights and wrongs were that created the rift in the first place, a huge amount of time has passed, and you're now considering what –if anything –you should do now.

"The second card relates to the essentials of the situation. You might call this the heart of the matter. We have the Fool in this position. This denotes someone who is naïve and innocent, and also rather stubborn. This person won't compromise or fit in, as he or she is following a different path. This situation often occurs when teenagers try to become more independent.

"The third card indicates anything that could prove helpful to you in resolving this situation. You have a powerful card here: Strength. This shows that you possess the necessary qualities of compassion, patience and tenderness to help resolve this situation. It also shows that no matter how hard or difficult the process might be, you have the necessary determination to carry it through.

"The fourth card is the Lovers, and this is in the unexpected or unforeseen area. This could denote an unexpected love affair, or it might indicate someone who is prepared to help you through this process. It could also relate to a choice you have to make. Does any of that make sense?" For the purposes of this reading, we'll assume that her brother has offered to help her contact her mother.

"The next card relates to your subconscious desires and wishes about this matter. The Hierophant in this position reveals your desire for a more spiritual side to your life. It also shows that you might meet someone who could help you gain a richer and deeper knowledge of yourself. At the very least, this person will give you good advice.

"The final card relates to a possible outcome. Temperance is a hopeful card in this position. It suggests that you be patient, as this matter will not be resolved overnight. However, with a bit of compromise, honesty, open communication and love, it looks as if you and your mother will be able to resolve the difficulties from the past, and start anew."

THE HOROSCOPE SPREAD

Like many Tarot card readers, I'm also interested in astrology, which probably explains why I like this particular spread. It's particularly useful when someone wants a general reading, as it covers every area of a person's life. There are twelve houses in astrology, each covering a different aspect of the person's life. After the cards have been thoroughly mixed, twelve cards are dealt out in a circle to represent each house. The first card indicates the First House and is dealt at the position of the hour hand of a clock when it's showing nine o'clock. The remaining cards are dealt in a counter clockwise direction, with the final card (the Twelfth House) being dealt at the ten o'clock position.

The areas of life each house covers are:
- **First House:** Personality, physical appearance, disposition, mannerisms, vitality and outlook.
- **Second House:** Money, finances, income, possessions, resources, self-worth and self-esteem.
- **Third House:** Brothers and sisters, short trips, writing, communication and the intellect.
- **Fourth House:** Home, mother, security, property and old age.
- **Fifth House:** Children, loved ones, creativity, entertainment, pleasure, hobbies and interests.
- **Sixth House:** Health, work, co-workers, service to others, food and pets.
- **Seventh House:** Partnerships, personal relationships, enemies, the public and legal matters.
- **Eighth House:** Legacies, inheritances, partner's finances and death and rebirth.
- **Ninth House:** Overseas travel, higher learning, publishing, philosophy, religion, intuition and spirituality.
- **Tenth House:** Career, occupation, ambition, attainment, public standing, reputation and the father.
- **Eleventh House:** Friends, acquaintances, associates, community work, hopes and wishes.
- **Twelfth House:** Unexpected difficulties, hidden weaknesses, secrets, secret enemies, and the occult.

If you spend about five minutes on each house, it will take at least an hour to do the Horoscope Spread. This is because the person being read for is likely to ask a number of questions about each house. For instance, they might ask, "Is my personality holding me back?" when you start talking about the First House, "Will I get a pay rise this year?" when you get to the Second House, and so on.

Extensive readings of this sort are extremely helpful to people, as they cover every aspect of their lives. However, they can be exhausting for the person doing the reading. Consequently, you shouldn't try anything as complex as a twelve card reading until you've gained experience with one, three and five card readings.

Sometimes, you might want to do a Horoscope Spread to answer a particular question, especially if the answer involves two or more houses. A few years ago, a friend of mine told me that he wanted to become a fulltime writer. He had had a few books published in the past, but none of them had been financially successful. He had enough money saved to survive for almost a year, which meant he could devote himself fulltime to writing as long as it paid off. It was a huge risk, as he had a young family and a large mortgage. I decided to use the Horoscope Spread as it enabled me to answer his question, and also see how his dream would affect other areas of his life.

His question was, "Will I be able to make a living for myself and my family as an author of mystery novels?" Answering this question involved at least five houses: the third house for writing, the fifth house for creativity, the ninth house for getting the books published, the tenth house for occupation and reputation, and the second house for making money from it. He didn't mention the possibility of becoming a famous author, which is a tenth house matter. There are other factors, too. What effect, if any, would this decision have on his wife and children? Would an irregular income stream cause stress and ultimately ill health? Would he need to travel to promote his books? It's possible to look at all twelve houses and receive information from all of them that relates to his question.

Here are the cards he drew:
- First House: Three of Pentacles
- Second House: The Sun
- Third House: Four of Wands
- Fourth House: Two of Swords
- Fifth House: Ace of Wands
- Sixth House: Three of Chalices
- Seventh House: Eight of Pentacles
- Eighth House: The Wheel
- Ninth House: Knight of Wands
- Tenth House: Ten of Chalices
- Eleventh House: Seven of Wands
- Twelfth House: Two of Chalices

You might like to lay these cards out in a circle, and give my friend a reading based on them. What do you think I told him? Do you think he's writing novels fulltime, or is he still working at his regular job and dreaming of becoming a writer?

THE CELTIC CROSS SPREAD

This is possibly the most famous spread of all. It was first published in "The Pictorial Key to the Tarot" by Arthur Edward Waite in 1910. He wrote: "This mode of divination is the most suitable for obtaining an answer to a definite question." Because this is the spread taught in most booklets of instructions that come with decks of Tarot cards, many people are familiar with it, and ask me to use it when reading for them. As you'll be asked this, too, it's an essential spread to learn. However, you should wait until you've gained some experience as a card reader, and are familiar with the other spreads, before experimenting with this one.

The main value of the Celtic Cross spread is that the cards gradually supply information that provide clarity and insight into the particular question. By the end of the reading, your client should have a clear understanding of the circumstances surrounding the question, and the likely outcome.

The first step is to choose a Significator card using one of the methods described earlier.   The Significator card is placed face up on the table, and the cards are thoroughly mixed, and then cut three times.

- The first card is then dealt, and placed face up, partially covering the Significator card. As you do this, say: "This covers you." This card provides clues about the nature of the problem.

- The second card (not counting the Significator) is dealt and placed face up across the first card, creating the Celtic Cross that gives this spread its name. As you do this, say: "This crosses you." This card reveals the type of obstacles that are likely to occur.

- The third card is dealt face up above the Significator card, as you say: "This crowns you." This card indicates the best possible solution to the problem.

- The fourth card is dealt face up below the Significator card, as you say: "This is beneath you." This card indicates the past influences on the client's concern.

- The fifth card is placed beside the Significator card on whatever side the person depicted on the Significator card is looking away from. If there is no person, or if he or she is looking straight ahead, this card is placed to the left of the Significator card. As you deal this card you say: "This is behind you." This relates to the immediate past.

Significator

1

3

10

Significator

1

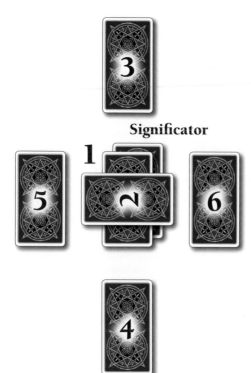

5

2

6

9

4

8

7

- The **sixth** card is placed on the opposite side of the Significator. This is the direction the person on the Significator card is looking towards. As you do this, say: "This is before you." This card indicates the immediate future.

The final four cards are placed in a line, one above the other, on the right hand side of the cross.

- As you deal the **seventh** card, say: "This is your Self." This indicates the person requesting the reading, along with his or her state of mind, feelings and attitudes.

- The **eighth** card is placed above the seventh card as you say: "This is your environment." This indicates the views of everyone else associated with the question.

- The **ninth** card is dealt above the eighth card as you say: "This represents your hopes and fears concerning this matter." A good card in this position indicates the person's hopes about the question. A negative card represents his or her fears.

- The **tenth**, and final, card is placed above the ninth card as you say: "This is what will come." This card indicates what is likely to occur. There is a temptation to immediately read this card and ignore the others. However, this card should always be read last, as it is the final outcome of everything that is depicted in the other cards.

As you can see, the Celtic Cross spread is more complicated than the others. However, it provides a great deal of information that can help the person decide what to do concerning his or her question.

CONGLUSIONS

—ᜠ—

SPIRITUAL GROWTH AND TAROT

Most people buy their first deck of tarot cards because they're interested in using them for divination purposes. However, many progress beyond this and use their cards to develop inwardly and spiritually. Tarot cards provide an extremely effective way to tap into your higher consciousness and gain enlightenment.

Meditating on different cards is a good way to start this process. All you need is ten to twenty minutes of uninterrupted time. You might want to temporarily turn off your phone. Make sure the room is at a comfortable temperature. Wear loose fitting clothes and make yourself as comfortable as you can. I like to sit in a recliner or upright chair, as I tend to fall asleep if I lie down on a bed. Do anything else that puts you in the right state of mind. You might like to light candles, burn incense, cover yourself with a rug, visualize yourself surrounded by a clear white light, or play some quiet meditation type music, for instance.

When you feel ready, take several slow, deep breaths. Allow yourself to relax more and more with each exhalation. Once you've done this, choose a card from your tarot deck. You might look through the deck and select a specific card. Alternatively, you might mix the cards and select one at random. If you have a special need, you might deliberately choose a card that relates to it.

Put the deck aside and study the card you've chosen. Look at it closely, and pay attention to the details you may not have noticed before. Look at the clothes any people on the card are wearing, and notice their facial expressions. Look at the background and pay attention to the buildings, landscape and cloud formations. Think about why certain animals are depicted. The snail in the foreground of the Nine of Pentacles is a good example.

Study the card for as long as you can. When you feel ready, imagine a beautiful frame around the card, and visualize it hanging on the wall in front of you. As you look at it, imagine it growing in size. It continues growing until it's large enough for you to step into it. Imagine yourself getting out of your chair and stepping into the Tarot card. Allow yourself to be drawn into the card, and become part of it. There's no need to will or force this to happen. Remain relaxed, and simply allow it to happen.

Once you're "inside" the card, allow the meditation to take you where it will. From this perspective, you'll find you can speak to the people in the card, walk along the same paths that they walk on, eat the grapes, dip your toes into the water, climb the mountain peaks, and do anything else that is in the particular card you chose. You can even mentally become one of the characters in the card, and gain insights into what motivates them, and how they think and talk. While you're inside the scene notice what aspects of it fill you with delight, and what makes you feel sad or anxious. One advantage of entering into the card is that you can see behind anything. You can look behind the throne of a king or queen, for instance, and see what's there.

Some people like to close their eyes once they're inside the card, as this helps their visualization. You can do this if you wish, or you might prefer to continue "living" inside the picture. It doesn't matter what you do. Likewise, some people feel they're actually inside the scene, while others experience it as if they were watching a movie. Some people close their eyes and don't see anything. However, they feel and sense all the sights, sounds and smells of the scene. Other people who also close their eyes visualize the card and wait for information to come into their mind. Everyone is different, and whatever feels right for you is the correct way for you to perform this particular meditation.

When you feel it's time to come out of the meditation, look around one last time and see if there's anything in the scene that you haven't noticed yet. Once you've done that, visualize yourself stepping out of the card and returning to your comfortable chair. Sit quietly for about thirty seconds. When you feel ready, slowly count from one to five, and gradually bring yourself back to your normal everyday world. Become familiar with the environment you're in, and then stand up and move around for a minute or two. It's a good idea to drink some water and to eat something after a meditation. I generally eat a handful of nuts and raisins.

As soon as possible after the meditation is over, write down your experiences in a journal. Record your feelings and insights, as well as everything you remember. All of these will be useful to refresh your memory when you read what you've written at a later date. It's possible that more insights will come into your mind in the following day or two, and you should write these down, too.

If you do this meditation regularly, you'll be amazed at the insights they provide. You're likely to gain increased self-esteem, and your intuition will expand. Your relationships with the special people in your life will improve, as you'll gain increased sympathy, tolerance and love. This meditation can be used for self-development as well as increased spiritual insight.

It's a good idea to do this meditation exercise with several cards that appeal to you before experimenting with cards you find unpleasant or difficult. The confidence you'll gain from the earlier meditations will help you handle the more difficult cards without any problems. If you feel doubtful about this, say to yourself, "I'm entering into this card with no stress, emotion or personal baggage," immediately before stepping into it.

If you're still in the process of learning the cards, you should do this meditation every day, if possible. By doing this you'll get to know and understand all 78 cards in less than three months.

—⁂—

CONCLUSION

I'm sure that by the time you've worked your way through this book, you'll be as much in love with your Tarot cards as I am. This book is intended for beginners, and once you've mastered it, I'm sure you'll want to continue learning more about this fascinating subject. The best way to do this is to explore different decks, as each one has its own energy and distinct personality. Fortunately, there are many different Tarot decks available. I have more than three hundred decks in my personal collection, but I'm inclined to go overboard with my enthusiasms. I still occasionally buy another deck, as I'm always curious to see how different artists "see" the cards. Because I have so many different decks, it's hard for me to recommend one or two to start with, but I do have two favourites.

If, like me, you're curious about what's behind the scenes in a Tarot deck, you'll love the "Tarot of the New Vision." This deck shows all the cards in the Tarot deck from the back, rather than the front. Another deck I use frequently is the "Wheel of the Year Tarot," as my clients respond well to the modern interpretations of each card. You should be able to find these, and many more Tarot decks, where you bought this kit. Recently, someone told me that there are many windows, or paths, to the Tarot, and that is why there are so many different decks. Every deck provides insights in their own particular way.

I find it helpful to use more than one deck when I'm meditating with the cards. Sometimes I'll look at the same card in several decks to see how different artists have portrayed them. At other times, I'll choose a particular deck because it feels right for me at that moment. I do the same when reading for others. I usually use the Universal Tarot, but always have a few other decks handy, just in case I feel the person would be helped more if I used a particular deck.

There are many good books that will help you learn more. Naturally, the more you know about the cards, the better you'll become as a reader. Reading different books on the Tarot will help you develop deeper meanings, and each author will give you additional insights into the Tarot. Some of my favourite authors on the Tarot are: Terry Donaldson, Mary K. Greer, Marcus Katz, Anthony Louis, Mark McElroy, Barbara Moore, and Rachel Pollack. You'll find all of their books will help you understand and learn more about the Tarot.

I wish you great success as a card reader. You'll find them extremely valuable for self-development and spiritual growth. You'll also be able to help many people with your card reading skills. You may decide to become a professional Tarot card reader. You may use your expertise to help your family and friends. You might use the cards to help raise funds for an organisation you're involved with. You might use them solely for yourself. Whatever you do with the cards, I know they'll help you in many different ways. I hope that one day you and I might be able to give each other a reading.